Jennifer,
Thank you
for hanging out @        2018
Workhuman        Nicole

# MindSET
# Your
# Manners

Nicole Gravagna, PhD

i

# DEDICATION

For everyone who taught me the lessons illustrated here. Frustrated moments were my classroom, arguments my recitations, and tears filled my inkwells. I sincerely hope you get as much value from these experiences as I have. I am forever changed.

# CONTENTS

# ACKNOWLEDGMENTS

Judith Orloff, M.Ed included me as a participant in a five month class called Disruptive Learning Technology. My participation in that program dramatically shifted my perspective about emotions, human behavior, and the world at large. This book is largely informed by what I learned there. Thank you, Judith.

To all of the people who allowed me to ask questions about their lives so that I might have stories to share, to preserve anonymity, I'll simply say, thank you. You know who you are.

For countless wonderful conversations about this book and related topics, thank you to, Chris Neale, Tony Tomassetti, Jake Winkler, and Travis Tallent.

And thank you to Tom Higley for writing S. E. T in his notes in large letters when I told him my ideas about sensation, emotion, and thought over breakfast. MindSET was born a few days later.

# Introduction

This book is not my story, but it is shaped by my story. This book is not about me because my story is small and this is as big as the whole world. I live in my own petri dish and the truth is that you, dear reader, live in your own petri dish too, so I suppose it's necessary that we start there. This story starts in the vast internal universe of yourself and ends in the universe shared by the whole world.

Welcome to your adventure. An adventure that, if all goes well, will illuminate the answers to your conflicts. This book isn't going to solve your conflict for you, any more than a map magically moves you from point A to point B. You will have to take the first steps and then keep going. You are the main character in your story. This adventure is a hero's journey.[1] It's the natural process that people go through to accept change.

---

[1] Joseph Campbell was a mythologist. In his work *The Hero with a Thousand Faces* in 1949 he suggested that all myths followed the same structure which we now call The Hero's Journey. The death that occurs during the journey is a death of the ego, an idea that he took from Carl Jung, a psychologist.

Fig. 1 - The hero's journey illustrated in emoticons.


**The Journey of You**

1. You receive a call to adventure
2. You initially refuse the call.
3. A supernatural aid makes it possible for you to accept the call to adventure.
4. The adventure begins and it must be your sole responsibility.
5. The adventure descends into painful and treacherous trials.
6. Death seems imminent.
7. Instead of a physical death, a death of identity frees you from the past and you are able to rise from the trials as a stronger, freer being.
8. No longer encumbered by the past, you return home where reintegration into family and normal life completes your journey.


When I started writing this book, I set out to tell the story of why change is hard. I wanted to rely on scientific evidence. I figured there must be something in the structure of the human brain that made it so difficult for us to accept change. As I researched the brain under conditions of change, a different story came to light. I discovered that conflict is intertwined with change. Sometimes conflict drives change and sometimes change causes conflict. Either way, conflict is in fundamental association with change. So, I looked deeper into the way the human brain deals with conflict.

Conflict, in its simplest form is just two competing ideas. What stood out to me was that the human brain can't think about two conflicting ideas simultaneously. We can't think about any two different things at the same time. Thoughts occur one after the other, not simultaneously. I have no suggestions about why this is. It's just a limitation of the way our brains work. To think about two things, you have to shift back and forth between them.

That's not all I found. When two conflicting ideas are presented to your brain, you can't stop thinking about the disparate nature of those ideas. The brain doesn't rest until the conflict is reconciled or smoothed over in some way. We are wired to pay attention to conflict.

I studied the neuroscience of both change and conflict in hopes of finding some biology hack that we could all use to make our lives easier. I wanted to pull peer-reviewed biomedical journal articles together so I could share the measurable evidence of neuroscience data. Of course, I wanted this. I'm a trained scientist. As I continued on my journey of learning and writing about change and conflict, I realized that it was impossible to tell this story entirely through data. I learned that there's a difference between knowledge and knowing. Knowledge is the thing that you can capture in a book. Knowing is an experience that can't be found in books. With that understanding, I realized that I have given myself the impossible task of guiding you, dear reader, to *knowing* using only this book.

I am not so foolish to think that I can fully guide you through your journey. All I can do is share that there is something to know. Then, you must go about the business of experiencing it. This book is your call to the be the hero in your life's journey. It's a call to a new way of life. You will likely find a way to initially refuse this call, just like every person does on a hero's journey, but when you are ready, this book with provide you with a (seemingly) supernatural aid so that you can go on.

You will discover your own, real-life, trials that will push you deep into scary places. You must enter into those increasingly difficult trials and you alone are responsible for your success or failure. You will feel pain. You will slay old demons. You will expose skeletons that have been hiding in your closet.

Then, you will arrive at the final trial close to death. You won't have a corporeal death, where your body lies motionless with no vitality. That kind of death is not useful. Instead, you will say goodbye to, and mourn, a small part of your identity. That kind of death will be enough. When you rise, free of the weight of your past, you can return home.

# My Journey

There was something that I learned in a book that helped me see that there was some knowing to be had. I'll start there. My call to begin the hero's journey came from the book *The Charisma Myth* by Olivia Fox Cabane. I had watched others maintain an admirable air of control in sticky situations and I knew that I wasn't capable of doing the same. At the time, I had recently moved from a scientific lab career to an office-based business career and I was a regular witness to my own distinct lack of grace in business meetings. I wanted charisma, if for no other reason, than to feel more comfortable in my own skin.

I read *The Charisma Myth* in hopes that I would learn how people manage their emotions, handle difficult questions, and generally keep their poise under fire. The book succeeded in giving me the information that I needed, but it didn't offer the answer that I wanted. I was hoping to learn tricks like eye contact, posture, and word choice that would convey charisma. Cabane, the author, instead gave me the call to my hero's journey. She shared that there is no trick to having charisma. To project warmth, power, and presence, you have to actually possess warmth, power, and presence. Her book told me that charisma was the natural side effect of letting the world see who you really are deep down. Charisma required authenticity, which is what happens when your inside matches your outside.

I was floored. *The Charisma Myth* called me to change the truth of what was inside, so that I could project my genuine self in public. I couldn't do that. I imagined how business meetings might go if people knew what was going through my head. My thoughts were not generous or kind. I'd be fired in minutes. I refused the call.

The supernatural aid that pushed me to go forward with my journey might be surprising. I was wrapping up a business meeting, thinking that I had done a great job of hiding the way that I felt about everyone in the room. Someone from that meeting was helping me gather cups and papers off the table and he said, "I can tell you have a hard time with this." His comment cut through my illusion. I sincerely thought that I was hiding my feelings. This man, a stranger, could see right through me! He had a supernatural power of reading my mind.

I felt violated and naked. It quickly occurred to me that this man was not special. Everyone could see through me. Everyone knew how I felt on some level. I understood why charisma was so powerful. We each possess the power to see others' secret inner self that is thinly veiled from the world. When the inner self matches the outer self, the resonance is strong and beautiful. We can feel the strength and beauty in that person. When the inner self and outer self don't match, the person you see is a conflicted mix of both selves. It's much harder to see the strength and beauty of another person through their attempt to hide how they feel.

My journey began with that violated feeling I had when I realized the world could see what a jerk I really was. I set out to become the person inside that I wished to portray on the outside. I had no idea how I was going to accomplish that change.

People knew me as smart, serious, and the kind of person who always got the job done well. After more than a decade in academic research, I became the operating head of an angel investment group called Rockies Venture Club, then later I became a management consultant for a boutique firm, after that I built a distribution company that sold medical devices. I did high quality work, and people liked me, but there was something blocking my ability to build and maintain tight relationships with clients. I didn't know it then, but it was the conflict between my inside self and my outside self that got in the way.

I kept putting myself in intense roles where I was good at the technical elements of the job and nervous about the human elements, and I started to worry that I might destroy myself with the stress of it all. Hard jobs were so attractive that I couldn't resist them. Instead of dialing back my work ethic or choosing easier jobs, I decided I'd have to get better at managing my reaction to stress. Interactions with other people kept coming up as a repeat source of stress, so I decided I'd start making personal improvements by trying to understand my fellow human. I wanted to be a warmer person. Warm people smile, which was something I didn't do, so I thought I'd start there.

It would not have been a hero's journey if I had been able to start smiling one day. The hero's journey includes a series of trials that are intense and challenging to overcome. It's not that smiling was a forgotten habit. I actually couldn't do it. It was a big deal. People I met socially would routinely come to the realization that I didn't smile. With their recognition of this fact, they seemed pleased to have discovered the source of what I can only imagine was a feeling that something was off about me.

Each trial of the hero's journey comes with its own moment of initial refusal. For a long time (a few years) I denied that I needed to smile. Yes, I wanted to be warmer. Yes, I wanted to be authentic. Yes, I wanted to be good at relationships. No, I didn't need to smile. I figured there must be another way to get along in life. I was in denial. I had every excuse about why I didn't need to smile. Here's a few examples. I'm from the East Coast where nobody smiles. My parents don't smile. I'm a scientist and scientists don't smile. You can't smile and think critically at the same time (I don't think this is true, but I heard myself say it once.)

A shift in my perspective helped me to end the smile embargo. I learned that other people can feel the emotions that I express and when I wasn't smiling, I wasn't expressing joy. The realization hit me. The smile is a side effect of feeling and expressing joy. A smile doesn't matter on it's own. Smiling is just a measurement of whether I am able to express joy. I had been able to convince myself that I didn't need to smile, but I was not willing to go through the rest of my life without outwardly showing that I felt joy. How depressing I must have been! I felt joy, but kept it hidden deep inside.

My perspective shift came from a class I took, led by a woman named Judith Orloff, M.Ed.[2] Judith had been my business client in the past, and she contacted me out of the blue to join a pilot class she was giving. I joined the class because I was in the early stages of writing this book and I hoped that I might learn something that I could include. Judith became my guide for the rest of my hero's journey. What she taught me changed my life forever, and has deeply informed this book.

When I set out to understand what made change hard, I didn't know what I would find. I uncovered some themes as I studied human challenges. I noticed that conflict was a common element in change. Conflict either preceded or followed a change in someone's life. I noticed that change always had some element of uncertainty. You simply can't know how a change will affect your life. Often a big change in someone's life caused them to question who they were in light of that change. Identity, then seemed like a big part of change. Finally, it was impossible for me to ignore that change brings on strong emotions. Change, is therefore, not a purely logical thing. Without knowing what significance these notions might hold (change, conflict, uncertainty, and emotion), I gathered them up and began to research how they affect the brain.

I was giddy when I discovered that in all the research, there was one part of the brain that was associated with all of these elements. The Anterior Cingular Cortex (ACC) was active when a person changed their mind. The ACC is part of the pathway that allows you to decide if you will act out an emotion. It's the part of the brain most commonly implicated in recognizing conflicting information. The ACC is active when you have to make a decision and you feel like you don't have enough data to go on. I was in search of the part of the brain that allows a person to gracefully manage change in life, and the ACC started to look like an outstanding candidate.

The ACC seemed like a thermostat of sorts. A thermostat constantly measures the temperature in the room and when the temperature is outside of a set range; it then acts as an automated switch to turn on a

---

[2] I include Judith's educational credentials because there is a highly visible woman by the same name with a medical degree, whom I have never met.

heater or air conditioner. In a similar way, the ACC has information passing through it much of the time, but only when a specific threshold is crossed, does the ACC tell the rest of the brain and body that it's time to act. I started to think of the ACC as a box with a simple job of sounding the alarm when needed. In my imagination, the alarm shouts, *Do something!* It maintains a threshold that, when crossed, sounds an internal alarm and inspires a person to act.

I thought about myself sitting in a business meeting, all the while I'd be listening and taking notes. Then all of a sudden someone would say something that triggered an internal alarm inside me. My brain would start screaming, *Do something!* My thoughts would scramble to figure out what to do. My body would react with tense muscles and sweat. All along, it was my ACC that told me it was time to freak out.

It occurred to me that the real difference between people who can handle emotions, conflict, uncertainty, and change gracefully might be the people who have figured out how to calibrate the threshold in their ACC. Those people are less sensitive to pain and stress than everyone else. For many years, I had wondered how some people were cool and collected under fire. For the first time in my life, I had hope that I too, might be able to manage my reaction to emotions in times of high stress. Maybe, all that I needed was a better handle on my ACC.

## Stories of Change

To write this book, I needed stories of people who had found an easier path to change after they calibrated their ACC. I couldn't just google *calibrated ACC*. How could I connect with people who were capable of quieting the voice in their heads that screams *Do something!*?

While my own ACC was uncalibrated, I wasn't able to handle a routine meeting without having a conflict between the self I wanted to portray and the one that I'd rather hide. So, I had at least one willing test subject - me. I would follow my own progression from a high-stress reactionary person to someone who could manage situations consciously. A book about one person's journey could be interesting, but I knew this book needed more than just me as a test subject. I meet a lot of people and fortunately, I was able to find a few additional willing test subjects who also wanted to learn how to stop being reactionary to conflict and change. Some people chose to remain anonymous; they have been given pseudonyms so that their stories could be presented throughout the book. Others were willing to let me use their real names. Generally, the brave souls who allowed me to share their stories are people who have a public following through their companies, blogs, or social media. Feel free to follow their ongoing journeys as they keep posting and sharing their future trials.

Many of the stories are unfinished because they are real stories from real people. Some stories are of people getting stuck in an attempt to change. Those people were actually stuck at the time this book went to print. Of course I care and worry about them, but the hero's journey is driven by the hero alone. All I can do is be available as a mentor and guide, I can't push them through their trials. They must be responsible for their own success.

I wanted to include stories of people who have lived exceptional lives by following the lessons that are outlined in this book. Obviously, they didn't learn how to live exceptional lives by reading this book. I found people who were living with low stress, not because they were living easy lives, but because they had figured out how to manage stress in spite of doing hard things. I included those stories to illustrate just how grand life can be without an internal fire alarm going off all the time. I met some of these people serendipitously, and others I contacted specifically to involve them in the book.

You'll notice that many of the stories are from entrepreneurs. I looked to the lives of entrepreneurs to illustrate some points about change. Although there is the opportunity for change in everyone's life, entrepreneurs seem to eat change for breakfast. They change company affiliations and job titles faster than children need new shoes. They run companies that grow and shrink and switch gears to sell a new products. They hop from one field to another, reinventing themselves each time. I chose to write about the lives of entrepreneurs you may have never heard of, instead of retelling the stories of Richard Branson or Elon Musk.

Initially, I thought that I could look to entrepreneurs to discover the secrets that allow a person to manage change. What I learned is that entrepreneurs are masters of two things: identity and uncertainty. When I looked into how humans deal with uncertainty, I discovered that the spookiness of uncertainty drives most people's decisions in a way that isn't particularly logical. Was it possible that a calibrated ACC could help people manage uncertainty just like it helps us manage stress and pain?

I watched Chris Neale, the CEO of Fracture ID, an oil and gas technology startup, go through the uncertain process of raising $2M from venture capitalists during the writing of this book. I spoke with Claudia Batten, co-founder at Massive Inc. which was purchased by Microsoft for a few hundred million dollars, who learned how to use uncertainty to her advantage. Finally, I learned from Tom Higley who was the CEO of Service Metrics, a company that was sold only 18 months after it was founded and turned 27 of its employees into millionaires.

The whole world has become more entrepreneurial than it was just a few year ago. Millennials are switching job as fast as entrepreneurs do. They hop from one field to another and learn to be comfortable with the discomfort of uncertainty. A side effect of moving around a lot in your career is that you must be able to manage your identity. To tell the stories of young people living in a changeable world, I connected with a few students and recent graduates. Kiara Imani Williams is a young person who has embraced a fluid identity. She calls herself a millennial, a beauty queen, and a journalist with a law degree. Another story came from Melissa who is an undergraduate at Case Western. She made the identity switch into becoming a woman in technology (also known as a software engineer) during the writing of this book.

Finally, I included stories from Michael and Susan Simpson. They spent years in post-Soviet Russia coaching and teaching ethics and communication skills to people who had been abruptly thrust into a completely new way of life as the whole country privatized. Change is something that is very personal, even when it is forced upon us in a systematized way.

# Conflict

I set out to write a book about change and, as I dug into my research, I discovered that there was a bigger story here. Change isn't hard. Uncertainty, shifting identity, modifying beliefs, stress, and emotional pain, these things are hard because when we encounter them, they are the cards that we are forced to play whether we want to or not. Ready or not, you have to make a decision. The thing that forces your hand is conflict. Conflict is the real story.

The human brain is wired to pay attention to conflict even when we don't consciously know we are experiencing a problem. Conflict hijacks the brain and triggers mental rumination, which is the annoying experience of thinking about the same thing over and over again without wanting to do so. When you are lying in bed awake, stressed, and unable to get your mind off a topic long enough to go back to sleep, that's conflict. There's nothing inherently wrong with a little conflict, but the problem lies in our biology. When there's conflict, we can't think about anything else.

Getting away from conflict frees your mind to think about whatever you want. Without conflict, you are more attentive, aware, and capable of meeting your goals. You can be compassionate toward others without having to vie for self-preservation. You can look at the world with wonderment and an appetite for learning new things. Those gems of charisma, warmth, power, and presence are traits that naturally exist in you (and everyone) when conflict isn't distracting you. Authenticity is easy when you aren't engaged in a continuous fight about who you want to portray to the world. Without conflict, your thoughts and feelings are perfectly acceptable to share publicly without censorship.

To escape conflict, you must go through a hero's journey of your own. This is your call. Deny, reject, turn back, and get it out of your system. It's time for you to see what the world looks like when you aren't consumed with conflict. This is a big deal and it's a journey not to be taken lightly. Your trials will be personal. You will be forced to question whether you've understood the world at all. Have you got it all wrong? How badly do you want to find out?

# How to Use this Book

The body of this book is a guide that will show you the paths and pitfalls of conflict. You will learn where conflict comes from and how to get past it. You are ready to start your hero's journey when you are ready to see what your life is like without the continual background noise of conflict. Without conflict, your life will be different in some ways and the same in other ways. There's no way to know what will change and what will remain the same. When you are ready to push forward with the uncertainty of what will be, then you can be successful.

MindSET is not a new set of skills that you have to learn. It's actually a very basic set of skills that you were born with. Everyone has them; these skills come standard with the human body. Unfortunately, we learned other skills that move us farther and farther away from using our MindSET. You have had, all along, the skills to navigate the world, connect with others, and let go of conflict. If you are ready to return to those roots, you can unlearn the lessons that are no longer helpful. Ready?

## Exercises

Each chapter includes exercise boxes. When you encounter a box, you can choose to stop reading and do the exercises. Alternatively, you can keep reading and do the exercises later. You will find that some of the exercises are valuable for you and others don't help you much. Highlight those that serve you well and do those exercises as often as you need to keep your ACC calibrated.

You can involve friends and family in the exercises too. Ask others to read the instructions for you so you can close your eyes during the exercise. Or you can act as a guide to help others calibrate their own ACC. If you have children, you can guide them through some of the ACC calibrations to help them get past fears and anxieties. These exercises can work for anyone.

# Journaling

Journaling can be either writing, drawing, or recording video. You may find that it is extremely helpful to document your thoughts as you go through this book. By the time you reach the end of the book, you'll have the skills to get out of conflicts, but you'll wish that you went through the book with a conflict in mind. It can be hard to choose which conflict you want to work through initially. You might not know which is the most important conflict. Journaling can help you get around this conundrum.

When you document your thoughts, you leave breadcrumbs for yourself. You will unwittingly leave clues to what's important. Some part of your mind knows what's important even if you don't know consciously. When you've learned all the skills in the book, you can go back through your writings or videos and see what matters to you. You'll be able to follow the breadcrumbs and uncover your conflicts at that point.

# 1: CONFLICT

*Conflict is the beginning of consciousness*

M. Esther Harding

Michael Simpson[3] found himself in a conflict with a shopkeeper. Michael didn't need to be fluent in Russian to understand her message; she was angry. She seemed to be angry at him.

What had transpired moments before was an attempted transaction. Michael wanted to buy some everyday things at the corner store. He gathered his items, put them on the counter, and the next thing he knew, the shopkeeper was angry. She refused to take his money, glared at him, slammed the cash register drawer, crossed her arms, and looked away. He was befuddled.

Michael was an American living in Russia. He had been there for a few years, but was still struggling to fully understand the language, although he was making progress. The culture remained an even bigger question mark for Michael. Winston Churchill called Russia a riddle wrapped in an enigma, inside a mystery. Michael's reasons for being in Russia were

---

[3] I'm using a naming system that distinguishes between people who I personally interviewed (first, last then resort to first in subsequent references) and people whose stories came from other media (first, last then resort to last in subsequent references.) A third naming system is used for people I interviewed, but who would like to remain anonymous (pseudonym first names only).

personal. Michael had followed a love interest. Spoiler alert: He gets the girl.

Michael and Susan met when they were 26 years old in Atlanta, Georgia and he fell in love immediately, but she did not. Susan moved to Ukraine to work with a faith-based organization invited by the Russian Ministry of Education to re-establish a foundation of ethics and morals. Initially, her mission was to teach at a business school in the catastrophically messy, post-Soviet Kiev, Ukraine. Susan didn't stay in Ukraine. She was frustrated that her dependence on translators prevented deep conversation, so a year later she moved to St. Petersburg, Russia to study Russian and continue her work. Susan was professionally connected to the business of understanding the enigma that was the Russian people.

Eight years after Susan moved to Eastern Europe, Michael moved to Russia to join her. For much of his time in Russia Michael wasn't formally working with Susan's organization, but he was familiar with the ways of American corporate life so he did contribute to the work they were doing in the ministry. And so it was for about six years, the two of them worked and lived in Russia together. They have since returned to the United states, and they say that their time abroad was life-changing and influences every aspect of their work and relationships to this day.

Fortunately for Michael, Susan was with him when the shopkeeper lost her cool. Susan was able to talk the woman down after her emotional response to a simple, everyday situation. After some discussion, they learned that it was Michael's choice of payment that threw her into a tizzy. He was paying more than he owed, which meant the shopkeeper would have to give him change. Not a lot of change, mind you. He had 500 rubles on the counter (about $20 at the time) and he was expecting about 350 rubles in return. It was this fact that ruined the shopkeeper's mood.

Ideally, Michael would have understood the problem. He would have been able to show compassion to the shopkeeper in spite of her behavior. Maybe he would have been able to alter his behavior so there wasn't a problem. He could have bought more items, or he could have searched his pockets for a smaller coin. Michael however, was stunned and didn't do any of those things.

The shopkeeper wasn't used to people being cooperative. She was used to fighting. The culture of Russia at the time (1990s) was full of fights. Michael saw signs of abuse regularly and not just in a "bad" part of town. He said violence and aggression seemed to be normal. Underhandedness was normal. Lying, stealing, and cheating were all expected behaviors. Life had gotten difficult in Russia leading up to and after the fall of the Soviet Union and most of the people living there had gotten used to doing what they had to do to live. At the peak of violence, right around the time Michael was in Russia, the homicide rate was three times higher than it was by the time things started to settled down around 2011. Alcoholism, embezzlement, drug use, and drug trafficking were all rampant in Russia around the same time.

Business practices and government policies were corrupt and full of clashing rules and laws. Tax law was impossible to follow. Everyone had to lie and cheat as a matter of course. It's not that it was a nation of bad apples, it was a broken social structure and you could trace a lot of the problems all the way up to the policies that were in place under government leadership. Corruption in governments and businesses trickled down to personal life. Conflict was everywhere. Michael experienced the conflict himself when he attempted to buy groceries and ended up with a fight. Was the shopkeeper crazy from living a hard life? Not at all. She had a real struggle going on and Michael walked right into it.

So why did the shopkeeper get upset about having to give Michael 350 rubles? She didn't have the change and that wasn't her fault. The shop owner, her boss, made a habit of coming by every hour or so to remove the cash from the register. Anyone who runs a brick and mortar business in the United States knows that in the morning you start the day with $200-250 in the register. The distribution of that money is such that any transaction will allow the shopkeeper to make change. At the end of the day, you balance the register back to the starting amount and take the rest of the money to a safe or bank. But that's not how they did it in Russia. Keeping enough change in the register was not the practice. Shopkeepers would start the day with about 500 rubles and as the money built up in the register, they would ease into the freedom to make change when necessary. After a few hours, shop owners would arrive to harvest the money, again leaving the shopkeepers with little to make change. The shopkeeper had a perpetual problem of making change for customers.

The shopkeeper's anger was well beyond what you might expect for a person enduring even the most annoying business practice. She was livid and it was personal. The shopkeeper was *in reaction* and her emotional state had little to do with Michael. Michael just happened to walk into a hornet's nest of conflict. The shopkeeper likely had conflicts associated with her job, her family, and her neighbors. There was a lot going on with her, and most of the people in Russia at the time. Michael and Susan had a saying they heard to explain what they saw in Russia. They said, "Hurt people hurt people" meaning that when someone is hurting, they tend to cause pain for others. So, where does the cycle begin? Can it be stopped? Is it possible for the shopkeeper to ever feel better? Is it possible for a whole community or nation to heal?

## What is Conflict?

For Michael and the shopkeeper, conflict looked like displeasure and confusion. Sometimes conflict is less dramatic. Conflict can be a simple misunderstanding like thinking that dinner reservations were at 6, but having to wait for your table until 7. Conflict can seem hopeless like working for minimum wage, but wanting to drive a fancy car. Sometimes conflict can be hard to define like when you can think of 35 different reasons that you dislike going to work in the morning.

Conflict occurs when you have a belief that doesn't match your experience. You anticipate one thing and another thing happens. The human brain naturally registers when two thoughts don't agree; this biological response is the foundation of conflict. The biological term for conflict is cognitive dissonance. The brain has a dissonance detector and it can be very sensitive. When something doesn't make sense in light of what we know to be true, we stop and give it our full attention. We will inspect the conflicting thoughts until we can reconcile the discrepancy. It can be as simple as these equations.

$$1+1=2 \text{ (Yes)}$$

$$1+1=3 \text{ (Wait, how?)}$$

Cognitive dissonance is highly motivating. It's uncomfortable to have something on your mind that doesn't add up. When you experience conflict, you spend time and effort trying to reconcile it. Conflicts inspire mental processing which is why the equation 1+1= 3 will capture your attention much longer than 1+1=2.

Our brains are wired to be attracted to conflict. We are like this, even at birth. Babies can't resist the attention-grabbing allure of conflict either. Scientists measure a baby's attention by tracking eye movements. In a series of experiments designed to measure infant attention, scientists put a ball on a stage where a baby could see it. When the baby was looking, they lowered a curtain and replaced the ball with a stuffed dog behind the scenes where the baby couldn't see the switch. Then the curtain was raised and the baby saw a stuffed dog where the ball was supposed to be. The cognitive dissonance created by the switch caused the baby to stare measurably longer. When a ball was replaced with an identical ball, the child didn't bother looking for very long. You can interpret that the switch is interesting to the baby or annoying to the baby but either way, the scientists captured the baby's attention by creating a mismatch. It's impossible to know what the baby is thinking, but it's clear that there's something going on and the baby takes time to process it.

Conflict requires mental processing that creates measurable delays in cognition and action. These delays mean that you are not as mentally quick when you are dealing with a conflict as you are when you are free of conflict. In real life situations, dealing with conflict steals your attention from the things you'd rather be focused on.

Conflict creates delays in mental processing and action in two ways. Conflict simply captures your attention. Just like the baby, you will think longer about something when it seems different than you expect it to be. You can imagine how dangerous it might be when you are driving a car, to have your attention on a conflict instead of the road. You often see secondary car accidents that occur nearby a big accident on the highway. People pay attention to the conflict instead of their driving and this results in fender benders.

The other way conflict creates delays in processing and action is by continually attracting your attention back to the conflict, for hours, days, or weeks after the initial problem occurred. Imagine that you were reprimanded at work and that your mind kept going back to that situation over and over for the next week. That conflict keeps drawing you in. Pulling your mind away from the conflict is hard, but life goes on and you have to be able to pay attention to what's going on in the present. It takes effort to shift your attention away from conflict, and pay attention to the present. Often, your mind takes over again, and your attention is back on the conflict.

It would be fine to have a conflict brewing in your mind if it were possible to go about your business and forget about the conflict while you were doing important things, but that's not how the human brain works. The human brain is amazing in all it's capabilities, but one thing it can't do, is think about two things at once. The brain can only think about one thing at a time.

Multitasking is a misnomer. What gets labeled as *multitasking* is actually task switching or the brain going back and forth between more than one thought or activity. You can type an email and talk on the phone at the same time, but your brain is switching back and forth between the tasks like a railroad car switches between tracks. The switch takes time and during that switch-time, your brain is momentarily offline. So typing an email and talking on the phone at the same time takes measurably longer than doing each separately. The more switching between tasks that you do, the longer each task takes to complete.

When your brain is working out a conflict, the conflict is an irresistible task for your brain. Any other task that you try to accomplish while you have a conflict has to compete for mental bandwidth with the brain's desire to pay attention to the conflict. Each time you pull your attention away from the conflict you devote a little time to that switch. If you give your mind the slightest break from the desired task, it will shift back to the conflict. When you realize you've lost ten minutes to daydreaming about the arguments you might have used to defend yourself in your last fight, you snap back into the present. Each time you switch between the conflict and the task you want to be doing, you lose a little time on the switch and switch back.

Conflict is a time-waster, but it also *feels* terrible because it activates a part of the brain that also deals with pain. The anterior cingulate cortex (ACC) activates when the body feels pain and also when the brain determines a conflict. Think of this part of the brain as a checkpoint to determine what action, if any, is necessary. When something happens, the ACC decides whether you need to *Do something!* When pain occurs while cooking, a prudent action might be to retract your hand from a hot pan. When a conflict occurs, a prudent action might be to fight back, change a course of action, or do nothing. The ACC helps you determine your behavior. The discomfort associated with pain and conflict are thought to act as motivators. If the conflict were comfortable, you wouldn't deal with it, you'd just let conflicts happen which could ultimately result in injury or death.

The mental processing caused by conflict is both uncomfortable and uncontrollable. It's like having a lack of control over your own mind. Psychologists use an elegant test called the Stroop Test to measure time lost to conflict.[4] A Stroop Test creates a conflict for a subject using words on a page. Though used extensively in psychological tests to study how the brain handles conflict, it's been used for serious international matters as well. During the Cold War, American Intelligence used the Stroop Test to catch Russian Spies.

Suspected spies were shown a paper with the Russian words for red, blue, yellow, and green. The Russian word and the color of ink that the word was printed in were different. Anyone who could read Russian, would experience the conflict between reading the written word and the color of ink. Those subjects were measurably slower at naming the ink color. For people who could not read Russian, there was no conflict. They could read the color of the ink without being influenced by the meaning of the word. Even though their lives depended on it, the Russian spies could not help but let the conflict of words and colors slow down their responses. Conflict caused the spies to lose control over the time it took their own minds to process the task. This measurable delay caused by processing conflict is called the Stroop Effect or sometimes the Stroop Conflict.

---

[4] This test was published by John Ridley Stroop in 1935, though he got the test from German scientists. The test is well documented and the results have been replicated more than 700 times.

**Exercise: Stroop Test**

Get a watch or use the timer on your phone.

Test 1: Read the ink colors quickly aloud. Time yourself.

Grey Black White White Black Grey Black White Black Grey Black
Grey White Grey Black Grey White Grey White Grey Black White
Grey Black Grey White White Black Black Grey Black Black Grey

Test 2: Read the text words quickly aloud. Time yourself.

Grey Black White White Black Grey Black White Black Grey Black
Grey White Grey Black Grey White Grey White Grey Black White
Grey Black Grey White White Black Black Grey Black Black Grey

Subtract the time of test 2 from the time of test 1.

- The difference between the two times is the measure of time that you processed the conflict of the written word and the ink color.
- A short time delay means that you were able to get through the conflict quickly.
- A long time delay means that you took a long time to process the conflict.

If a simple conflict of text meaning and ink color can create a measurable delay in your ability to act, imagine what a true-to-life high stakes conflict might do to your ability to concentrate. Your brain gets bogged down processing conflict. Since we encounter simple and complicated conflicts multiple times a day, every day, you can see that conflict is a significant use of human brainpower and processing time.

## What Conflict Looks Like

Conflicts that create problems in real life feel a lot more complicated than 1+1=3 and the word *white* written in black ink. Real life conflicts include frustration and hurt, emotions, and history. Real life conflicts also include fears about the future and unresolved issues from the past. Like Michael and the shopkeeper, real life conflicts seem impossible to boil down into a simple solution. The shopkeeper was hurt from a lifetime of living with fighting and corruption. Is it hopeless to heal conflicts in a person who has so many wounds? Fortunately for humanity, it's possible to clear up conflicts in even the most deeply wounded people and it doesn't have to take a long time. But in order to clear up conflict, you will need to understand it.

One type of conflict occurs when you have an experience that doesn't jive with what you know to be true, and you have no control over that experience. Another type of conflict occurs when your behavior doesn't jive with the behavior you expected to exhibit. Put another way, there are two ways to find yourself in conflict: 1) when your belief of the world doesn't match with your experience of the world and 2) when you don't perform how you expect to perform. These two kinds of conflict feel different. In one case, you feel like you are butting heads with an outside force, like another person. In the other case, you feel like you are butting heads with some outside force that prevents you from performing the way you want to. In reality, both types of conflict are completely within your control.

## Experience conflicts

Here's an example of a conflict I experienced myself a few years ago. Like most people raised in the United States, I believed lemons were yellow. This simple belief got me into a conflict that nearly damaged my reputation. I was having lunch with a scientist from Mexico. She was prominent in her field, which was the field I was in at the time. I was nervous and trying to impress her and found myself doing exactly the opposite. I gave the impression that I was a stubborn person who had to be right.

We ordered lunch and she asked for a Coke with lemon. When it arrived, she looked disappointed and pulled the yellow fruit out of her drink tossing it on a napkin. I was interested in pleasing her so I asked what was wrong. She responded with a hand wave that signaled, oh never mind, and said she had wanted the green lemon in her drink. Ideally, I would have listened to her talk about green lemons, and asked her about her experience with lemons. With an open mind, I could have learned a lot about citrus fruits around the world. She was a prominent biologist after all. But, I did not have an open mind. Instead, I had a belief about the color of lemons and it caused a conflict for me.

Two pictures came up in my head. Lemon is yellow. Lime is green. She said lemon was green therefore she's wrong. My brain ran in circles to make sense out of the conflict. I knew that the fruit on her napkin was a lemon, and she had asked for a lemon, but she insisted that the fruit on her napkin wasn't what she had ordered. She wanted a green fruit called a *lemon*. The apparent conflict caused me discomfort and uncontrollable mental activity. My first attempt to reconcile the situation was to correct her English. I assumed that she was adorably confused in her translation of Spanish to English. I'm embarrassed to admit that I corrected an accomplished scientist about the name of a garnish.

She corrected me back. "That's not a lemon," she said, pointing at the lemon on her napkin. I started to wonder if she was an argumentative and stubborn person. I was ready to write her off as an unshakable academic when the waiter gracefully stepped in to save us both. He overheard our argument and he stopped by to clear up the confusion. In Mexico (and other Latin countries) the fruit called *limón* is green and the fruit called *lima* is yellow. He went on to say that in Spain, the limón is yellow and the lima is green, but it wasn't always this way in Europe. The Spanish painter Luis Meléndez created "bodegón con limas" (Still life with limes) in 1760 and the painting features a yellow fruit. At some point the names of the two fruits were confused and the confusion propagated into entire regions of the world. It's unclear which way the fruits were named originally so there's no point in trying to figure out who is right. Both fruits bear both names.

Fortunately, we were able to move on to discuss other issues like our research and the lemon/lime debacle was gracefully shifted into the past. There was no harm done and we had a nice lunch. However, I nearly wrote off a prestigious scientist as a difficult person and she might have been doing the same with me. Maybe she was right; I was acting like a difficult person. The yellow fruit was a lima or lime and my insistence otherwise was a conflict for her. In my mind, I put her down. I judged her reaction and I decided her English was unpracticed. Yikes.

The conflict occurred because I chose to adhere to a belief about lemons instead of listening to the person in front of me. Listening doesn't include agreeing or disagreeing. Listening isn't about doing anything at all except taking in information and encouraging more information to flow. I heard her say *lemon* and when it created a conflict, it was in that moment that I had a choice: be open-minded or insist on being right. I could have recognized that she was talking about things outside of my knowledge, in which case I would have adopted an attitude of listening and learning. Instead I made sure that I connected her statements directly to what I knew to be true; I adopted an attitude of judgement. My choice of attitude was not ideal for relationship building.

The lemon/lime conflict was a simple example of a conflict which is seemingly caused by someone else. I couldn't control my lunchmate's choice of words and the conflict threw me into reaction. I corrected her English which is not a behavior I'd choose if I were acting like myself. There was no harm done in this situation, and it easily blew over. Imagine, however, if the person across the table from me wasn't a visiting scholar who was essentially a stranger, but instead that she was my sister. Imagine that we had a lifelong history of getting into battles over things as simple as fruit. A little argument over a lemon could put me into reaction and then she could go into reaction and before long, we would be shouting and digging up old sorrows from years prior.

Conflict can be a little hassle or it can be a really big deal. When conflict is a hassle it takes energy and time, and it's uncomfortable. When it's a big deal, it can damage relationships and get people hurt or even killed. So, what's the difference between hassle and big deal? Conflict diffuses when people are able to control their actions. Remember the ACC, the part of the brain that activates when you experience a conflict and also when you experience a pain? That part of the brain allows you to determine what action you'll take, if any. When you feel a stone in your shoe, your ACC makes a judgment call to determine whether you'll tough it out, or whether you'll sit down to remove the stone. When you feel a conflict, your ACC makes a judgment call to determine how you'll deal with the situation.

Many conflicts occur because of an external event that you can't control. Remember at the heart of the conflict is a belief about the world that isn't jiving with your experience of the world. You might not be able to control your experience, but you can control your belief. You will learn how to manage your beliefs so that you can be free of conflicts. Keep reading.

## Integrity conflicts

Conflict is not always triggered by other people or external events. You can create conflict for yourself. When you fail to live up to your own standards, you feel it as a painful experience. We tend to notice the big failures like getting fired, failing to quit smoking, failing at a relationship, or closing a business. However, there are a million little failures that lead to the big failure in performance, and those little failures can be prevented.

When you fail to perform to your own standards, you have endured a slip of integrity. *Integrity* simply means wholeness. Integrity is about having no unfinished business. It means that you set out to do something and you did it. Sometimes people use the word integrity as a judgment about morals, but that's not the way it's used here. When you find yourself in an integrity conflict, you either set yourself up to accomplish something impossible, or you failed to follow through on something possible. Either way, your brain wrestles with the open-endedness of the unfinished business.

This unrest in your brain is called the Zeigarnik effect and it was named after psychologist Bluma Zeigarnik, who first noticed this phenomenon. She saw that people were better at recalling information from something unfinished than they were at recalling information from something finished. The Zeigarnik effect has been blamed for causing intrusive thoughts, or thoughts you can't stop having, about unfinished business. When you don't behave with integrity, and fail to complete the things you start, your brain registers this as a conflict.

To prevent the Zeigarnik effect, it's important to finish things. Think of integrity as a complete circle and a lack of integrity as a circle with a piece missing. When you draw a circle and it isn't completed, you have drawn a line in the shape of an arc; you have not drawn a circle. A completed circle connects back to the beginning. You can finish things in many different ways. Finishing a project doesn't always mean taking it to the biggest fruition possible. Sometimes it means abruptly closing the circle.

Fig. 2 – Integrity simply means wholeness. Broken integrity creates feelings similar to conflict. The broken circle is less pleasing and captures your attention longer than the whole circle.

Here's an example from my own life. I submitted a proposal to the CEO of a company for a project that would take three months to complete. He didn't respond right away and as time moved on, I started making plans that would interfere with my ability to complete the work I proposed. To stay in integrity, I had to get a meeting with the CEO where I encouraged him decide whether we would start the work I proposed. He shared that it didn't make sense to begin the work this year; some things had changed since we last spoke. I thanked him and went on my way. If I had let that proposal sit on his desk without having that conversation, my brain would have had intrusive thoughts. I might have worried that he'd call unexpectedly wanting to begin the work. Instead, we discussed the proposal, and decided that we would not execute on it. I was free to go on making my own plans without the Zeigarnik effect taking up my attention. I closed the circle abruptly.

It's very common for people to start things and not finish them. A lack of integrity is part of modern culture. Telling someone, "Let's do lunch," without following up shows a lack of integrity. Showing up late to a meeting or appointment with no prior warning also shows a lack of integrity. Deciding not to complete an assignment without discussing it with the other people involved lacks integrity. Deciding that you are going back to school, but then doing nothing toward achieving that goal is a failure of integrity. We all lack integrity at least a little bit each day. It adds up. The Zeigarnik effect is a self-inflicted conflict that creates uncontrollable mental activity and distracts you from the things you would rather be thinking about.

Ideally, you will be able to seriously consider the beginning and the end of each "circle" you start before you start it. If completing a circle seems like it is not within your capability, then the responsible decision would be to not start that circle in the first place. In more concrete terms, if you know it will be impossible for you to arrive to a meeting on time, you would tell someone that you will be late.

George Lucas' wise character Yoda[5] has been quoted saying, "Do, or do not. There is no try." To act with integrity, you do what you say you will do. There is no *try* in integrity. The moment you hear yourself saying, *I'll try*, then you know you are not acting with integrity. When you make closing circles a priority, it becomes easier to be honest about what's possible.

When Yoda uttered those famous words, he was teaching Luke Skywalker (who was on his hero's journey at the time) how to move stones using only his mind. Luke didn't embrace that it was possible for him to do this task. He said he would try. Try is not the same as do. For Luke to accomplish the trials in his hero's journey, he needed to be in integrity. He didn't have the luxury of having a distracted mind full of intrusive thoughts caused by the Zeigarnik effect. Luke had to focus.

You are on your hero's journey too. To get free of the conflicts that bog you down, you will have to find presence of mind. You can't focus when you have a lot of unfinished business on your mind. As you become more responsible about the circles you start, you will stop the creation of circles that are impossible for you to close. Then, you will close the circles that you have open. Through this process, your mind will naturally clear. You will find that your attention is sharper and you have more control over what you think about.

When you live without integrity, you often do so with the best of intentions. You try very hard to accomplish the impossible. You try to avoid disappointing anyone. You try to get across town in record time. You try to be superhuman in your efforts. Unfortunately, you succeed in

---

[5] The ACC shouts, *Do something!* To which Yoda responds, "Do nothing, I will."

creating a lot of unfinished business for yourself. You create distractions that don't allow you to perform at the best of your ability. You are much more capable when you live in integrity. Living in integrity is much more enjoyable than living without of integrity. Not only do you get to escape the conflict of the Zeigarnik effect, but you also get to have a closer relationship with those people you were afraid of disappointing.

How might someone living in integrity deal with a business meeting when they are certain they will not make it on time? If they are certain they can arrive to the meeting within 15 minutes of the start time, they would offer, "I will be 15 minutes late to this meeting. Is that ok?" By asking for confirmation, "Is that ok?" It opens the conversation for the other person to give more information. They might suggest that you skip the meeting entirely since the first 15 minutes will be crucial to understanding. They might agree to the late arrival time and agree also to share information about your scheduling conflict with the other attendees. They might agree to start the meeting later so that you won't miss anything. When you make a habit of sharing your limitations and capabilities with people, they do their best to help you. They might even save you a seat.

---

**Exercise: Closing Circles**

This exercise can help you take stock of the things you've left unfinished.

To begin: Get out your journal. Alternatively, you can use a phone app that records to-do lists. Make a list of everything you've been meaning to do. Include the tiny minutiae like scrubbing behind the soap dish and the huge bucket list items like learning how to surf or buying a home in a foreign country.

Go through and decide which items you can do this week with an asterisk. Be honest. Only mark them if you are willing and able to follow through. Then mark the ones that you are certain you will not work toward achieving this year by crossing through them with a single line.

If you were a waiter at a restaurant, how many tables do you think you could serve at a time? Write that number here _____.

You are left with a list of near-term, but not immediate to-do items. Now, picture each one of these items as a person sitting at a table in a restaurant. You are the waiter. You are responsible for that item. If an item sits on your list for a long time, it's like a person sitting at a table for a long time. You have to pay attention to it. It's easy to pay attention to things that are actively progressing like a person who is actively ordering and eating food. When there's not much action, like when someone decides to wait for a friend at a restaurant, you still have to pay attention to him. Your near-term, but not immediate to-do items take more energy than you may realize.

Do you have more to-do items than the number you wrote above? If so, consider making your list of ambitions smaller.

How this works: Each item on your to-do list creates an open circle in your mind. Just like a waiter has to pay attention to each table, you have to pay attention to each open circle. Everyone has a limit to the number of things they can care about at any given time.

Pitfalls: Overly ambitious to-do lists put your brain in a state where any additional conflict seems overwhelming. Open circles feel like conflict even when things are going well. To lessen the load on your ACC, limit the number of circles you have open at any given time.

---

# Managing Your Own Behavior

You'll discover that you can finish things when you are willing to do so. Most of the circles you habitually left open in the past were things that you could have completed. When you left those circles open, you didn't realize it was contributing to a lack of focus and overall lack of behavior control in your life. When it comes to the little things, it will be easier for you to start acting with more integrity now that you know what a lack of integrity is costing you. But what about the hard things? Everyone has a few behaviors that they know they'd like to stop doing, and yet it seems so hard to control yourself.

Emily[6] is one of the people who joined me in going on her own hero's journey during the writing of this book. Emily had a behavior that she

---

[6] Pseudonym

couldn't stop doing. She had a habit of interrupting others during conversations. People who worked with her and knew her socially waved off the behavior as a quirk. They said she was intense and spunky and they figured her conversational style was part of that package. Emily herself was aware of the behavior. People had dropped hints to her throughout her adult life about how she interrupted them. She knew it wasn't a positive behavior and she wanted to stop doing it.

Interrupting became a topic of conversation in couples therapy when Emily and her wife, Kelly, began having trouble communicating. Emily knew that she wanted to change her behavior and Kelly's frustration gave her the impetus to make it happen. But she was struggling. She caught herself wanting to interrupt in nearly every conversation. When she controlled her behavior she simply waited for the other person to stop talking before she started talking. She was just biding her time. She wasn't listening. She was simply holding her tongue. Sometimes she found herself focusing on her own breathing instead of interrupting. Although it seemed like an improvement on the surface - she wasn't cutting people off mid sentence anymore - she was checked out of the conversation, which isn't a behavior conducive to communication any more than interrupting.

Emily was going into reaction in conversations. A person in reaction isn't able to listen and is compelled to perform whatever behavior they have learned to perform under those circumstances. In Emily's case, she learned to interrupt when she was in reaction. It was a behavior that was acceptable in her family growing up. As a strategy to stop interrupting, she taught herself to focus on her breathing which is something she taught herself to do to control stress. In reaction, Emily's two learned behaviors (interrupting and breathing) were benign actions. She was not a danger to herself or society, but she was a terrible listener. When Emily was in reaction, she wasn't taking in new information. In conversation, she was missing the end of most people's statements. In discussions at home, she was missing a lot.

Emily said she wanted to stop interrupting and she was having trouble closing that circle. It wasn't a simple thing for her. It was a hard thing. Since she was going into reaction, she knew that there was a conflict and if there was a conflict, that there must be a belief underlying that conflict. To find that belief, Emily started noticing when she went into reaction. It was a little awkward for her to notice herself doing something undesirable without acting on it, but she knew that noticing without acting was an important part of engaging her brain's ACC so she could take control of the situation and stop going into reaction.

Noticing without acting is the first step to ending conflict. You can think of your ACC as a machine that you can calibrate for reaction. Left uncalibrated, your brain gets more and more sensitive to reaction over time. When you calibrate it, you can stay out of reaction and control your own behavior. Noticing without acting is an exercise in calibration. It might seem weird that doing nothing is so important to your brain's ability to function, but that is how it's wired.

---

### Exercise: Noticing Irritation

This exercise can help you start noticing the nuances in how external events or people affect your state of being.

To begin: Notice something in your home or office that bothers you. Maybe it's a stain on the wall or a sock on the floor. It might be a long to-do list or a noise that won't stop. Focus on it and feel the way it bothers you. Let it bother you. Give in to the irritation.

Notice any muscles in your body tense up. Notice your facial expressions. Notice the thoughts that arise in your mind. Perhaps you have some frustration with the person who made that stain or left that sock or increased your to-do list. Notice any emotions that arise. Do nothing about the thing that bothers you. Wallow in the irritation.

How this works: Your ACC takes a cue from you about what's important and what's ok to let slide. When you ignore your irritation, you don't give your ACC a chance to weigh in. By wallowing in irritation, and then taking no action, your ACC gets the message that your sensitivity to irritation is too high. Next time, you will be less sensitive to the same stimulus.

Pitfalls: There's a difference between deciding to do nothing and doing nothing. Deciding to do nothing, is actually doing something. It's deciding. To really do nothing, you simply notice the irritant in the room and notice your reaction to it. Then move on with your day.

---

Emily noticed that she was going into reaction in conversations every time she didn't understand what someone was talking about. In a discussion with Kelly about emotions, Emily didn't understand Kelly. Instead of taking that lack of understanding as a cue to really listen to her partner, Emily went into reaction and either interrupted or proceeded with her breathing techniques. You can imagine that Kelly would get frustrated. Halfway through conversations, her wife checked out! Emily wasn't acting with malice. She was going into reaction and couldn't help herself.

After Emily noticed a pattern of going into reaction when she didn't understand something, she was able to see the importance that she placed on understanding everything. According to Emily, her ability to understand was the most important part of any conversation. The irony of the situation wasn't lost on her. She realized that when she went into reaction, she stopped taking in new information and at that point she had zero chance of understanding what the other person was saying. She precluded any possibility of understanding because she so desperately wanted to understand!

When you are looking for the beliefs that underlie your conflicts, it can be helpful to think of them as black and white. All or nothing. The beliefs that cause the most trouble have a tendency to fall into the all or nothing category. Emily asked herself if she believed that she had to understand *everything*. She swirled with emotion when she found herself saying "Yes!" even though she knew it was absurd and impossible to understand everything.

Beliefs come from lessons learned. Most of the lessons people learn happen in childhood or teenage years. Some lessons are learned later in life, if a person drastically changes their lifestyle or has a trauma. Often, beliefs can be traced back to early lessons. Emily looked back to her childhood and life in her home. She said that she could remember getting a spanking for not understanding the consequences of something. She could remember countless situations where she was expected to understand.

After reflection, she found herself defending her need to understand. This was Emily's defense and denial. Remember that all hero's journeys include the phase where they reject the invitation to go on. She came up with four different ways that this belief was important to who she was as a person. It helped her in her job as a training coordinator. It helped her learn new things and stay up on current events. It helped shape her identity. Finally, it helped her connect to people she loved - or so she thought. She panicked when she thought about who she might become if she let this part of herself go. The hero's journey includes a moment when it seems as though the hero might die. Emily wasn't in danger of an actual death, but she was fearful that letting go of her belief might kill a part of her identity.

For a moment, Emily was torn and she felt a wave of panic wash over her. She wanted to stop interrupting. She wanted to be a better listener, but she didn't want to change who she was. She didn't want to lose the curiosity and inquisitiveness that made her special. This debate is healthy and if you will likely find yourself having a similar debate when you find a belief that you might choose to let go. Your beliefs are yours to keep if you so choose. It's all up to you. Emily pressed on. She saw what her conflict was doing to her marriage. She wondered if she could still be herself, curious and inquisitive, if she weren't compelled to understand everything. It didn't take Emily long to realize that if she weren't compelled to be curious, she could choose to be curious whenever she wanted to be. That realization helped her come to the conclusion that she was better off letting go of her belief.

Each time Emily didn't understand, she noticed her reaction. Noticing a reaction is about noticing how your body feels, noticing what thoughts race through your head, and noticing which behaviors you are compelled to perform. Noticing is a form of self observation where you act like you are an objective observer. She very consciously did nothing but notice herself go into reaction. This approach was different than when she focused on breathing exercises during conversations. She wasn't trying to escape the experience of going into reaction, she was noticing it. She let reaction happen and did nothing more. After a few times of doing this, the reaction got less and less intense. She started finding it hard to feel her reaction. After the third or fourth time of noticing herself going into reaction, the reaction was pretty much gone. Instead, she was left with an open experience of being able to listen even though she didn't fully understand what the other person was telling her. She discovered that not understanding was a little bit fun because she got to exercise her imagination to make sense of things she didn't get at first.

Controlling your own behavior is an important part of getting along in the world. Sometimes, your behavior is out of control because you haven't made a decision to control it. This choice is common for people who don't yet see the value in keeping with integrity. Living with integrity is a choice. No one has to do it. When you choose to live in integrity, you clear the way for being able to focus on whatever you think is important since your brain is not busy with conflict.

Controlling your behavior can seem impossible when you are in reaction. Being in reaction makes you a little bit crazy. While in reaction, your behaviors are seemingly unreasonable to others and you don't take in new information from the world around you. To control behaviors that are triggered by being in reaction, you can use a process of noticing, and ultimately letting go of the belief that causes the reaction in the first place.

# The Trouble with Beliefs

Conflict is a time waster. It's uncomfortable and it can inspire you to do and say things that are damaging to your relationships. Conflicts can't exist without beliefs since a conflict is an experience about the world that defies your belief about the world. When you have a belief about the world, you have a confidence in the way the world works. So, conflicts happen when you are confronted with evidence that your understanding of the world is not true.

We create beliefs because they allow us to feel like we understand the world. The choice, then, is to live in the uncomfortable state of not knowing what's going to happen or to create beliefs that might sometimes be wrong. Most people take the choice of creating beliefs that might sometime be wrong. Are we doomed, then, to a life of conflict?

The answer to that question is no. We are not doomed to live in conflict. To avoid that fate, you have to learn how to manage your beliefs so that when you are confronted with a conflicting view of the world, you can accept it. You can eventually get to a way of thinking, where you recognize that your beliefs are not true, and conflict becomes a thing of the past. To get there, you have to get a handle on how you deal with an experience that causes conflict.

When I tell people about beliefs and how they cause conflicts, they usually wish for some kind of assessment to tell them all of their beliefs. If beliefs cause so much trouble, why not uncover them and recognize them as wrong? Then you could go on with your life, conflict free. Unfortunately, it doesn't work that way. Even if I were able to give you a list of your beliefs, you couldn't just accept them as wrong. This is the hero's journey because it's hard to change your beliefs, they are the basis of everything you know to be true. How could you live your life if you dropped them all at once?

Beliefs feel as true as laws of nature.[7] *Gravity pulls objects down when I let go of them.* This is a law of nature. You know that it is true. It is true for everyone on the planet. Beliefs feel just as universally true, but they are not. Your beliefs are unique to you. They are not true for everyone on the planet. Others may agree with your beliefs, but those beliefs do not affect everyone. Imagine the moment when you discover that you've been living with a belief and treating it as truth, but now you see that it is not a law of nature. It's jarring to have that discovery.

When your experience is in direct confrontation with a belief, you will initially hold tight to your own belief. This reaction is normal. You built your beliefs to understand the world and anticipate events. All of your beliefs are based in some element of truth, so it can feel scary and dangerous to question them. You might be concerned that you will have trouble distinguishing between your true beliefs and your false ones. Don't worry about that. You can take some comfort in knowing that a belief is never totally true. The trouble with beliefs is that they can never completely match your experience, no matter how close to the truth they are.

---

[7] The Hidden Brain, and NPR Podcast, has an episode about how our hidden beliefs about the world affect our personal views of politics. For this episode search on Episode 44: Our Politics, Our Parenting. It originally aired on Sep 12, 2016.

Here's why. A belief is a thought -- a cognition. It's something you can put into words and it can exist entirely in words. An experience is more complicated than a thought. An experience includes emotions and sensations in your body like sights, sounds, and changes in your heart rate. No matter how close to truth your beliefs get, they can never fully match an experience. It's like comparing apples and oranges. They will never match. Therefore a belief is always a little bit false.

Some people struggle more with the disconnect between beliefs and experience than others. If you have rigid beliefs, you will struggle more with your experiences. If you have flexible beliefs, you allow for the natural disconnect that occurs on a daily basis. Transitioning from having rigid beliefs to flexible beliefs can be as easy as learning to liberally apply the word *sometimes*. There's a big difference to your brain when you give it the option of flexibility by using the word *sometimes*.

You can change the belief, "Successful people have a lot of money," into "Successful people *sometimes* have a lot of money." The change is subtle, but it means a lot to your brain. When an idea is concrete, your brain struggles any time you experience something that doesn't perfectly fit the mold. With the liberal addition of *sometimes*, you can save your brain a lot of conflicts.

Start limbering up by making your beliefs a little more flexible. This flexibility will serve you well on your hero's journey. By the time you have completed your trials and are ready to head back home, you will have confronted and retired at least one belief. These trials won't be easy, but they are worth while. Everything else in your life gets easier when you don't struggle with conflicts.

# Summary of Key Concepts

- Conflict occurs when you have a belief that doesn't match your experience.

- The Anterior Cingulate Cortex (ACC) is the location in the brain where conflict registers. The ACC also registers pain, which is why conflict feels terrible.

- Conflict steals your attention away from the things you want to think about.

- The two types of conflict are experience conflict and integrity conflict. Experience conflict feels like it is caused by an outside force. Integrity conflict feels like an outside force is causing you to behave in a way you would rather not behave.

- Integrity is simply about wholeness; finishing things you start, being responsible about promises, and getting closure for projects that seem open ended. Integrity prevents the attention stealing power of unfinished business, know as the Zeigarnik effect.

- When you are in reaction, you can't listen or take in new information. To get out of reaction, you can use a process of noticing your behavior and feelings.

- Beliefs are easier to manage when they are flexible.

# 2: History and Science of Conflict

*...but you don't have to take my word for it.*

Levar Burton

The irony of this book is that it's about clearing conflicts, but it will feel like the book itself is full of conflicts. You will have moments where it seems like you have to take some of these words as a leap of faith, or ignore them as contradictory to everything you know. I proffer a third option. Your experience of the world and the notions in this book can exist in harmony. What you see depends on where you are, both literally and figuratively. Two people standing less than a mile apart can spend all day arguing over the location of the end of the rainbow. If you've ever tried to find the end of the rainbow, you know that it keeps moving as you move to find it. The way the rainbow looks to you is different than it looks to someone standing away from you because the existence of the rainbow is an illusion made of tiny prisms of light shining through moisture in the air. The image of the rainbow depends on the angle of the sun, the moisture in the air, and the location of the viewer.

In the same way that a rainbow will look different to everyone, the world will look different to everyone. Every person's experience filters through their own conflicts and preoccupations. Imagine your conflicts are like water droplets in a mental sky that exists in your mind. As the sun passes through, you see your version of the rainbow, which depends on how close you are to your conflicts and how many there are. You will have a much easier time reading this book if you can accept that there are as many versions of reality as there are versions of the rainbow. None of those versions are wrong.

When you are confronted with a perspective that is jarringly different from your own, you can wonder what set of water droplets in the mind allows for that other view to exist. You can also wonder what you might learn if you were able to see that other perspective in your own mind.

# Very Old Conflicts

How can this book offer a new method of getting rid of conflict when people have been dealing with conflict for thousands of years with little to show for it? None of the philosophy in this book is actually new. People have had ways of clearing conflict since ancient times. What *is* new in this book is the compilation of scientific evidence that support the methods described here.

Brain imaging techniques perfected in the 1990s allow us to see into the brain. We can see which parts of the brain are active under different conditions. We can also see how brain activity differs from person to person. When you know what's going on in your head, it can be easier to see how conflict affects you.

Prior to the invention of brain imaging technology, it was impossible to see what was going on in the brain. Now we know how your brain reacts when you listen to your favorite music. We know what parts of the brain are firing when you feel anger. We can distinguish between PTSD, bipolar disorder, and traumatic brain injury with a functional scan.

Brain scan technology has become commonplace as a tool to understand the brain's activities. I visited Cerescan, a company that scans people's brains to help them diagnose disorders that are invisible beyond the difficulty that their patients have with daily life. I stood in a small room with a technician staring at a three dimensional brain on a screen. I squinted and tried to understand what she was looking at. She knew how to read these scans because she saw patient scans every day. The pictures were new to me. I saw a small dark patch on one side of a brain and asked about it. The technician waved her hand with disregard. "Oh, that's a little part of the brain that was killed by herpes simplex virus. You know, cold sores. Just about all the scans have something like that." My jaw flew open as I stood there dumbfounded. I knew cold sores lived in neurons, but I was impressed that we could see that level of detail in the scan. The tech went on to show me the distinct differences between the ADHD brains and PTSD brains and I left the Cerescan office convinced that we can see all ranges of fine detail in the functional regions of the brain.

For the skeptics and cynics of the world, a group of people nodding along with a guru is weak evidence of truth. There are too many spiritual and business gurus spouting their versions of reality. So, people tend to look to science as hard evidence. However, science is limited in that it cannot actually prove anything. It can only lend evidence toward one direction and away from another. Scientists never prove hypotheses. They either disprove them, or find evidence to support them, which is not the same as proving. There is much to learn, however, from many of the philosophies that both scientists and gurus have written over the centuries to help humanity find a comfortable and happy existence. I hope that the science presented here can help tease apart the quackery from the truth. MindSET is a way of processing conflict that was created from observing ancient philosophies through the lens of present-day neuroscience.

MindSET was developed using a broad understanding of human behavior that includes knowledge from 400 BC, scholarly work from before the industrial revolution, developments in psychology that occurred between in the 1940s and 1960s, economics research from the 1970s, and brain imaging techniques invented in the 1990s. Put all of that together and we get a very good picture of human nature, uncomplicated by the trends of the day or specific living conditions. By including studies of human behavior over a very long period of time, we can draw some conclusions about what's possible for any human whether rich or poor, sovereign or victimized, technologically advanced or archaic.

Life is very different today in much of the world than it was just 100 years ago. Technology now allows for nearly all people to be connected no matter where they live on the planet. Connecting with your fellow human used to be a much bigger job. Now, with a simple tweet, email, or phone call, you can get the attention of nearly anyone. Seventy five percent of the world's population has a cell phone. If you find it hard to talk to someone, technology is not the problem. Although we tend to cite distance, time, and money as the barriers that stand in the way of people connecting, it's simply not true. Although you may have the means and freedom to talk with your family and friends everyday, you probably don't manage to do so. With the very recent invention of the smartphone, you have a choice to be close to someone or to keep a desirable distance. For the first time in history, it's obvious that the distance between two people in a relationship can be controlled by those two people. Time, miles, or money don't factor into closeness anymore.

Now, we have the flexibility to live nearly anywhere and do nearly anything for work. Upward mobility is at an all time high in human existence and we can travel all over the planet for a relatively small amount of money compared to the cost of travel in the past. You don't need to be the economic top 1% to interact with people who grew up in other parts of the world. Cross-cultural interactions happen every day for both social and business purposes. With all of this intermixing of people from different cultural backgrounds, we are forced to see that any given behavior, like making noise while eating, is considered rude in some places and polite in other places. Actions, behaviors, and manners are judged differently in different places and a globalized world is a mishmash of people who are trying to connect with each other in spite of those differences.

MindSET is about clearing yourself of conflict so that you can connect with anyone anywhere for any reason. When you can really listen, you don't need to study specific cultural guidelines ahead of time. You can communicate in a fundamentally human way without all the bells and whistles of cultural rules. With MindSET, you will be able to communicate without words when necessary. You will be able to know how anyone feels at any time just by seeing them, hearing them, or being near them. You won't need to plan what you'll say or how you'll say it, because you will be able to find the right thing to say in the moment. Your interactions will be based on what you get from listening to a person in the present, not based on what you were taught to do or say in the past.

The human need for connection is not new, but recent technological advances have allowed us to see that connection is not as simple as occupying the same space, or talking to each other. A person flying across the world to see their family and friends may find more connection with their seatmate on the plane than they do when they are embraced by their own family. What prevents connection? What allows for it?

The business world is full or articles touting the benefits of authenticity in leadership, but few seem to know what it means to be authentic. You can find many articles debating what authenticity is and just as many debating how authentic one should be.[8] We've lost touch with what it means to be ourselves. We create these outward facing selves that interact with the world and say the right thing and do the right thing and in the meantime our true selves get out of practice dealing with the world. Our true selves become private and separate from the rest of the world. The private self thinks and behaves in ways that are unacceptable in public and thus we question the value in being authentic, especially at work. The common mistake is to assume being authentic means unveiling the true inner self, as is, to everyone in the office. That is not what this book recommends. Instead, authenticity means developing the inner self so that it genuinely matches the outside self that you want to present to the world.

## Empathy and the History of Suffering

Imagine yourself in the days of kings and queens in feudalistic Scotland in the 1700s. You were born into a family that tended someone else's land and it was unlikely that you had any chance at upward mobility. Your family's social standing determined who you talked to, who you befriended, and who you married. You likely didn't travel very far from your home. You settled and made a family in the same town where you were born. Your world was small and you knew exactly what was expected of you. You didn't live very long and your daily existence was focused on survival.

The industrial revolution changed everything. Over a few hundred years, changes in social structures, economics, and technology changed human

---

[8] The idea that one can be occasionally authentic is absurd. When you find yourself choosing which moments to be yourself and which moments to pretend to be something else, that's conditional pretending, not authenticity.

lives dramatically. Society went from a very structured and rigid thing to a very fluid and flexible thing. Instead of being stuck in one town and one lifestyle for generations, people saw that their lives could change within a single lifetime. One person could be born in poverty and do well financially, thus changing their status, living conditions, and geography. The shift in economics from feudalism to capitalism drove these changes. We are now used to the idea of upward mobility. We know that any individual can change their quality of life by doing well financially. A few hundred years ago, the concept of upward mobility simply didn't exist.

Adam Smith was a scholar who wrote two documents in the mid 1700s that are still taught today in colleges. The *Theory of Moral Sentiments* and an *Inquiry into the Nature and Causes of the Wealth of Nations* are both fantastically long works that professors tend to summarize in a few PowerPoint slides. In the tomes, Smith describes what is now known as *capitalism* and *democracy*. Smith was a philosopher, not a journalist. His writings mused on the future possibilities he saw for humans, which were in contention with the actual way of life that existed in his time. To give you an idea of the state of technology at the time, railroads were rudimentary wagon ways where wagons were pulled by horses on wooden rails. The steam engine was invented during Smith's time and the first vaccine came shortly after Smith died.

What stands out about Adam Smith's writing is that he very clearly, and at great length, describes the human sense of empathy as a fundamental driver in the structure of economics and government.[9] His notion is that any human can sense another's pain as their own, and because of that, humans are driven to prevent suffering as much as possible not just for themselves, but for those around them. He didn't need neuroscience and brain imaging to tell him that he had the human ability to feel another person's feelings. He knew that watching another human suffer caused him to suffer as well. Another person's joy brought him joy. Moreover, it was obvious to him that all humans have this innate ability.[10]

---

[9] Neuroscientist V.S. Ramachandran has a TED talk about empathy, economics, and government. To watch it search on the title - The Neurons that Shaped Civilization

[10] For those keeping score, empathy is the first supernatural aid that will help you on your hero's journey.

Understanding how to use empathy is a fundamental skill in MindSET. When you can allow yourself to feel the suffering and joy of others, you can connect with people on a level that is simply impossible to attain otherwise. Empathy is a critical part of listening. You can listen to emotions without using words. Empathy works between two people who don't speak the same language. Until you understand that you can feel the emotions of others, it's easy to get confused about the source of your feelings.

I had a wonderful conversation with a coffee shop barista who spontaneously shared with me her story of the most intense empathy connection she ever felt. She was traveling in Romania and, as circumstance had it, she ended up staying with an elderly couple who spoke no English. She spoke no Romanian. The three of them had dinner together that night and told each other stories and laughed and cried and transmitted pure emotion across the table because that was what they had in common. The language wasn't shared, but the emotions were. The barista was convinced that her's was a unique experience that occurred because she was in a special part of the world where such things could happen. Empathy is not unique or rare. It happens every day, it's just that we are too caught up in logic and words and expectations to notice it.

Since humans have the powerful ability to feel each other's pain, it would make sense that humans would behave in a way that ends suffering and promotes joy, yet this isn't how the world works. How is it that we have the capacity to create suffering, when those actions simply cause more suffering for ourselves in the process? Where does suffering come from and how do human behaviors create or nullify it?

Going back in time much farther than Adam Smith, to the ancient east, Buddhism was built upon the idea that we have control over how much suffering we endure. Siddhartha Gautama, a warrior prince who came to be known as the Buddha, lived around 400 BC. He promoted a way of life that translates to "The Middle Way." Some call it a religion, but because there is no deity in Buddhism, it is, technically speaking, a philosophy. Buddhism has spanned many hundreds of years, and although the specific cultural details of the philosophy have evolved multiple times, the basic premise remains. Suffering is caused by human nature, and the way out of suffering is to recognize the pitfalls of human nature and stop subscribing to them. This is, of course, a simplified summary, but it begins to answer the question posed above: Why do humans create suffering if we can feel each other's suffering? Buddhism suggests that we create suffering as a default. The natural desire for permanence, ownership, and more joy than pain actually creates suffering. Then, our natural ability to feel each other's suffering spreads the disquiet from one person to another.

To escape suffering, Buddhist philosophy suggests that we accept suffering. This is a counterintuitive plan and therefore Buddhism makes little sense to most people. Who wants to just lay down and suffer? That doesn't sound like a very good life. It's a hard concept to understand, but the point is that fighting against something actually keeps it front and center in your life. Therefore fighting against suffering actually increases suffering. It's as though whatever object you fight against is forced in a boxing ring with you, simply because you decided it was the enemy. You put that enemy in the ring with you. You created that relationship. Whatever thing you choose as your enemy, debts, ignorance, injustice, violence, the decline of family values, racism, substance abuse, whatever it is, you force that thing to greet you every morning to do battle.

Buddhism is full of riddles call *koans* that don't make sense at first. For instance, consider the sound of one hand clapping. It's not a simple concept. Koans are paradoxes that are used to show how life doesn't actually make sense and trying to make sense of everything will also bring suffering. To help people tap into the non-logical parts of their brains, Buddhism uses an exercise called meditation.

# Meditation and the Brain

Meditation can seem like spiritual *woo woo* to the uninitiated. You might imagine a person meditating in a robe sitting very still for a very long time and you have no idea what's going on with them. What are they thinking about? What are they doing? We now know, through brain imaging, that meditation activates parts of the brain that are used to translate information between the sensations in the body, emotions experienced, and logical thoughts. Meditation is exercise for the brain. It's like pushups and crunches that train the brain to be stronger in certain regions. Just like everyone can start small and work up to pushups and crunches, everyone can start small and learn to meditate.

**Exercise: Goofy Meditation**

People mistakenly think that meditation is about sitting still and thinking about nothing. This is not a description of meditation at all! Clearing all thought and emotion is impossible for all humans; it can't happen.

To begin: You are going to use your imagination. Close your eyes and imagine that you are getting ready to meet a consummate know-it-all. This person works in a office high up on the 100th floor. Picture yourself as you leave your house to go visit him. Imagine the drive or ride there. Imagine the building. Picture yourself taking the elevator or stairs all the way up.

During the journey, you'll notice that your thoughts try to interrupt your ability to imagine. Let them interrupt. Those thoughts are the voice of the consummate know-it-all! They will attempt to distract you and prevent you from reaching the office on the 100th floor.

How this works: Your mind is a thought-making machine. You can choose to follow the thoughts, ignore them, or notice them. To make it up to the 100th floor, you can notice the thoughts as they come, do nothing about them, and return to your imagined journey.

Pitfalls: It's common for people to think that they are too distracted to meditate. Meditation is about letting yourself notice and do nothing about distractions. At first, you will be tempted to follow distractions. Then you will be tempted to ignore them. Instead, notice them, and move on.

Therapeutic meditation was introduced to the United States in the 1980s under the name *mindfulness* by an American named Jon Kabat-Zinn. He created a mindfulness program in the University of Massachusetts Medical School that was focused on helping chronic pain patients. Shortly, thereafter, the program became geared toward stress reduction. Kabat-Zinn studied Zen Buddhism with various teachers, and identifies as a scientist with a PhD in molecular biology. The University of Massachusetts' Mindfulness program was marketed as a scientific endeavor, not a spiritual endeavor, and eventually all connection to Buddhism was downplayed as much as possible. The program still exists today as the Center for Mindfulness in Medicine, Health Care, and Society.

People who engage in meditation or mindfulness exercises have reported improved focus and attention, less anxiety, less depression, a reduced experience of pain, less incidence of illness, less stress, and closer relationships. It might seem far fetched that the benefits of meditation would be seen both in the physical body and in the mental state until you discover that meditation engages the part of the brain that translates signals between the brain and the body. There are a lot of benefits to strengthening the signaling pathways between our ability to feel and our ability to think.

Neuroscience research shows that people who meditate regularly over a period of years have some parts of the brain that are measurably thicker and denser than the brain tissue of people matched by age, education, and income who don't meditate. Dense brain tissue is considered a sign of healthy, active brain tissue. The ACC, the part of the brain associated with conflict and The MindSET Method, is developed by meditation. When something doesn't add up literally or figuratively, this part of the brain is active. Meditation, strengthens this part of the brain that deals with conflict.

# Hacking Your Brain to Solve Conflicts

The MindSET Method is, at its core, a set of physical and thought exercises that allow you to better use your ACC to manage conflict. Why does this particular part of the brain matter so much? It acts as the control center for your conscious behavior. Not only that, but it allows you to regulate your behavior in relationship to the behavior of others. It also allows you to behave in a way that isn't based on instinct or prior training, but instead is based on your own conscious decisions of how you want to behave right now. The ACC is the part of the brain that allows you to overcome your own nature to behave any way that you wish.

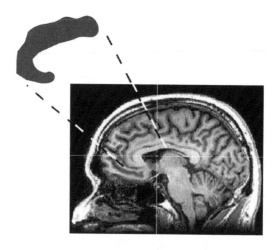

Fig. 3 – The anterior cingulate cortex (ACC). It sits behind the prefrontal cortex and wraps around the corpus callosum. The ACC is centrally located and has many connections between parts of the brain that deal with the physical body and the parts of the brain that deal with thinking.

MindSET is about making conscious decisions and acting them out through physical and verbal behaviors. When you are blindsided with news, how do you react? When you have to talk with a grieving co-worker, what do you say? When you are in the elevator with someone you've been trying to get a meeting with, how do you use those 30 seconds to your advantage? By strengthening the ACC, you will be able to say and do exactly what you want with no preparation at all, every time.

The ACC is critical to consciously controlling your behavior, and it has other functions too. Signals that pass through this brain area trigger a desire to act. When the ACC activates, it's like someone just hit your behavioral *On* switch. Consequently, you may find yourself running around like a chicken with your head cut off. Your ACC activates and you want to go! Even when there's nowhere you need to go. When your ACC is activated above a certain threshold, you get a loud and clear message from it. The message is *Do something!*

The ACC's message of *Do something!* is different than the fight or flight message that you may be familiar with. Think about the message *Do something!* as an early warning. *Do something!* is the fire alarm that goes off in the house when something is burning. If you took that fire alarm very seriously, you'd call the fire department (fight or flight). If you thought you could handle the fire alone, you might put it out yourself (take action, but not fight or flight). A third option is to take a good look at the fire and realize that it will go out on its own shortly. This final option would be equivalent to noticing the ACC's warning and choosing to override your innate desire to act. You get the message, *Do something!* and instead you assess that there's nothing you need to do.

Conflict activates the ACC. When you discover a conflict, you are driven to actively think about it or *Do something!* about it. Uncertainty also activates the ACC. When you don't have enough information, ironically, you are driven to act on that lack of information. When you do get enough information to update your view of the world or some small piece of it, the ACC activates then too. In other words, updating a belief, which is something you will do throughout this book to clear conflicts, also activates the ACC.

All of these things, conflict, uncertainty, and belief shifting, create a desire to start running around like a chicken with your head cut off. When you strengthen your ACC, you effectively calibrate the threshold at which your ACC shouts, *Do something!* Your brain learns to stop freaking out. Although we all have the instinct to *Do something!*, often there's nothing we need to do. When something is not going well at work, you don't need to freak out. When you are lost driving in a city, you don't need to freak out. When your partner acts differently than you are used to, you don't need to freak out. When you calibrate your ACC, you will be able to calmly notice that something is amiss without freaking out. You will be able to make necessary adjustments and get things back on track.

To solve conflicts, first you have to recognize that jumping into action in response to a conflict isn't helpful. That desire to act comes from your biology. It's the ACC screaming *Do something!* The conflict activates the behavioral *On* switch, not because you have to act, but because that's the path that a little electrical current in your mind has taken. Acting on conflict is a strong desire that gets us into trouble much of the time.

Each time you experience a conflict, you can tell yourself that it's just your ACC telling you to run around like a chicken with your head cut off.

Even after you know about the ACC's alarm, you'll probably do a little headless chicken dance anyway. It's a behavior you've been engaging in for a long time. It's ok to keep doing it. Now, as you embark on your hero's journey, put effort into noticing each time you run around like a chicken with no head. Get used to noticing how that feels. Watch yourself doing it.

In preparation for your hero's journey trials, you will want to raise your threshold for pain and irritation so that you aren't catapulted into reaction as easily. This is simply a matter of exercise that you can do over a period of a few weeks to measurably raise these thresholds. When people suggest that you get a thicker skin, this is kind of what they mean. Most events in life are not permanently damaging, and if you find yourself running into a lot of physical or emotional pain, then these ACC exercises will be very helpful.

## Calibrating Pain and Irritation

The ACC measures both physical pain and emotional pain, and when the threshold is crossed the ACC shouts, *Do something!* It's not that surprising that we would use the same word, pain, to mean both emotional distress and physical distress since the brain tends to treat them the same. What is physical pain anyway?

Basically, it's a sensation that inspires action. Pain says, *Do something!* It signals immediate danger to life or limb. A few babies are born with a rare condition that prevents them from feeling pain. These children are capable of breaking bones and continuing with their play as though nothing has happened. They have to learn to be vigilant of damage to their bodies in other ways such as making regular visual inspections of their own skin and joints. Many wear helmets. Pain is a fundamental part of living with a body. It keeps us safe.

Sometimes the pain response gets out of hand. You have certainly experienced a pain that seemed like an overreaction. Maybe you banged your knee or plucked an eyebrow too hard and it really hurt! Even though no immediate danger is present, you feel a strong sensation of pain. The body tends to overreact to minor damage. An oversensitive pain response keeps you safe and an under sensitive pain response can lead to physical damage.

The pain response can become so sensitive that it activates when there is no damage at all. Chronic pain is like this. A person with chronic pain doesn't have a current injury or unhealed physical damage, but the pain is still intensely present. Kabat-Zinn showed that meditation allowed people to calibrate their pain experience to interpret their pain differently. This reinterpretation happens behind the scenes in the ACC. It's not that you feel pain and consciously tell yourself it doesn't hurt: that would be more like fooling yourself into feeling less pain. What Kabat-Zinn did with chronic pain patients was to help them calibrate their sense of pain. The same sensation that registered as pain before the calibration doesn't register as pain afterward.

### Exercise: Irritation Calibration

Irritation can be a minor thing, but it tends to grow into frustration, anger, and resentment if ignored. This exercise allows you to be less irritated in the first place.

To begin: Sit very still in a safe place with your eyes closed and place your hands wherever they are comfortable. Don't move. Listen to the noises of the room. Look at the thoughts as they go by. Feel the sensations in and on your body. Go on a mental hunt to find something that is irritating you. It can be a thought or a sound or a feeling.

The easiest irritations to find are sensations. Sitting very still is guaranteed to create an irritation for you eventually. When you don't move, eventually something in your body will nag at you. It will beg you to shift your weight. It will beg you to lift your arm to scratch an itch. Don't do it! Let that pain or itch or irritation be. Let it grow into something you want desperately to relieve. Look at it. Feel it. Wallow in the irritation. Think about it. Imagine it growing so big that everything else is drowned out. Don't lose it!

Just kidding. You'll lose track of it. After you focus on an irritation for a while, it begins to melt away. You can't find it anymore. When that happens, you are done with this session of calibration.

How it works: Irritation is a signal to alert you to something. Once you've given your full attention over to the irritant, its job is done. It can stop irritating you.

Pitfalls: If you notice an irritant and decide that it's good or bad, safe or dangerous, then you've attached ideas to it. ACC calibration doesn't work on ideas, just feelings. Let any ideas fly by freely without connecting them to your irritation.

---

The normal pain response is an alarm that can also be calibrated. Without calibration, the threshold for the alarm gets naturally more and more sensitive over time. Athletes and people who do physical labor tend to get small injuries often. They have lower sensitivity to pain because they have raised the threshold at which they feel pain.

Calibration requires an experience of sensations that are both near and over the threshold of pain. Through conscious concentration, you can tell your brain to set a new threshold for which level of sensation is pain and which was just an intense sensation. Imagine getting a scrape while you are walking to work. You feel the sting of broken skin. You look down and think, "Oh well, I'll be fine." Each time you feel air against the scrape, you notice the pain and do nothing about it. You just calibrated your pain response to a higher, less sensitive, threshold. If instead, you stop what you are doing, inspect the area thoroughly and go through a process of cleaning and dressing the wound, you will lower your threshold for pain. Your ACC is looking to your behavior to tell it what is worrisome damage and what is a non-threatening incident.

## Feeling No Pain

Pain calibration is difficult when sensations are absent. Consider the plight of an amputee who feels phantom pain in a lost limb. After the limb is gone, there are no sensory signals coming from it anymore. The brain jumps to conclusions. When there is no sensation to calibrate, the brain decides that any and all stimulation from that area is pain.

You may be wondering how a missing limb can generate stimulation. The brain area that was associated with the now-missing limb has random neuron firings. In a healthy person these random brain firings might be registered as a twitch or odd tingle, but in an amputee, who has had no sensation from that body part in a while, the brain feels any stimulus associated with that body part as pain.

Calibration must be done in a different way when a limb is missing and no sensation from that area is possible. Phantom pain patients have experienced relief when doctors set up an illusion that makes it look like their limb has returned. Mirrors placed in just the right way can give the patient the temporary experience of seeing their limb in the right place again. They can mentally clench a fist or wiggle some toes with the missing limb and do the action for real with their opposite limb in the reflection. The illusion is enough for the brain. In a few minutes, the brain gets enough of a signal to calibrate the pain away for days or weeks.[11]

Emotional pain works in a remarkably similar way to physical pain. Emotional pain is a signal that crosses a threshold of action too. Emotional pain also shouts, *Do something!* Just like physical pain, the threshold becomes more sensitive when it isn't calibrated. We evolved to be this way. An ancient human who had an overly sensitive fear response about a rustling in the grass escaped snake bites and other deadly incidents. The overly fearful ancient human was probably wrong about a snake in the grass a lot of the time. He probably ran away from nothing fairly often, but his vigilance allowed him to live to pass on his DNA. In contrast, the not-so-sensitive ancient human who heard the rustle in the grass and didn't run away only had to be wrong once. It was a deadly mistake. Those ancient humans did not contribute to our gene pool. We now live in a world where we don't need to be as vigilant about life and limb as an ancient human. Our daily frustrations are not life threatening.

The threshold of emotional pain can be calibrated just like with physical pain. The calibration is just as easy. Instead of getting a physical scrape on the way to work, imagine getting a hurtful phone call from a friend on

---

[11] Neuroscientist Dr. V.S. Ramachandran gave a TED talk on this subject in 2007, which inspired Walter Reed Hospital to use mirror therapy as a routine approach to curing phantom pain.

the way to work. To handle this in a way that calibrates your emotional pain threshold, you have to first notice the emotional pain. You have to feel it and be conscious of it. Then, do nothing. The special formula of action here is to make sure your ACC is aware that there is emotional pain and then do nothing about it. Your ACC gets the picture. It starts to recognize that hurtful phone calls do not need to sound the alarm. There's no need to *Do something!*

When it's a physical scrape, the sensation still hurts no matter what you tell yourself, but by noticing the pain and telling yourself that you are ok, you effectively raise the pain threshold incrementally for next time. Do this enough times in a row and you measurably raise your pain threshold. This phenomenon has been measured in the laboratory. In the lab, a variable temperature probe is pressed against the skin on a person's arm to get a reading on a person's pain threshold. Very cold probes are painful no matter how much ACC calibration you've done. Sensitive people will report pain at a milder temperature and less sensitive people will be able to feel more severe temperatures without registering it as pain.

Noticing pain (either physical or emotional) is a necessary part of calibrating the ACC. You might be able to draw some parallels between phantom pain in amputees and emotional pain in people who tend to ignore their emotions. Phantom pain is the default reaction for the brain when it's not getting any sensation from the amputated body part. Might there be an emotional version of phantom pain? What does the brain do when all emotion is stifled?

Consider a person who has grown out of touch with her own emotions. This happens to nearly everyone on some level. It's easy to lose touch with what you are feeling. Parents of young children tend to stifle their emotions as they struggle through the challenges of parenting. Office workers tend to stifle their emotions in an attempt to act professional. People who have difficulties at home or at work may find themselves emotionally amputated after a while. There is no emotional feedback when you stifle emotions, and when there's no feedback there's no calibration. The brain starts to register every emotion as painful.

The amputees looked at a mirrored version of their limb and that was enough feedback to stop the pain response. The brain doesn't need much feedback. By noticing emotions in yourself and others, your brain is satisfied. You may need to start by noticing emotions in others first if you've become emotionally numb yourself. If you've been ignoring emotions, and you begin to notice them, they will be intense at first. After all, your threshold for emotional pain has been tuned to be very sensitive. With some time and regular noticing of emotions, you will calibrate the threshold to be much less sensitive. Then, when you have a high emotional pain threshold, you can experience all the emotions in a different way. Emotions aren't inherently painful. All emotions can be enjoyable when your emotional pain threshold is high enough.

Irritation has a threshold too, and like with pain, you can calibrate it. You may have been around someone who is particularly irritated with something that didn't even catch your attention. Or perhaps it's the other way around. You may find yourself irritated when others don't seem to understand your irritation. When your irritation threshold is sensitive, you get irritated easily. You might be tempted to use the exercises above to calibrate your irritation threshold the next time you are in public and someone just won't stop clicking a pen, or clearing their throat, or doing anything that drives you nuts. To calibrate your irritation threshold, you can't just tell yourself not to be irritated. That won't work. You must feel the irritation. You can feel your face crinkle in disgust. You can feel your shoulders tighten. You can feel the sour sensation in your belly. Notice how you can live through it all. You will never die of irritation. When you tell your ACC, by being conscious about these things, that all of this is going on, the irritation will diminish or disappear.

# The Neuroscience of Empathy

Emotion is everywhere whether you notice it or not. We can experience the emotions of others through our sense of empathy. Most people don't understand just how much information we are able to get through empathy and many are confused about how empathy differs from sympathy.

Sympathy is about recognizing that someone else is suffering. You may act to help the person suffering, and all the while you are feeling ok. Empathy is about feeling the suffering inside yourself. Instead of handing your crying friend a tissue and making a face of concern (sympathy) you physically feel her sorrow in your body and you will likely begin to cry too (empathy).

Empathy isn't limited to sadness. You can watch someone eating a delicious meal and you can start to feel like you are participating in a delicious meal too. Your mouth might even start to water. Could empathy be the basis for the success of cooking shows? Without consuming a single calorie, you can experience the pleasure of a beautiful soufflé or chicken cordon bleu.

Empathy requires activation of the Anterior Insular Cortex (AIC). The AIC, is directly connected to the ACC. When a person has damage to their AIC, they have a limited ability to empathize with the feelings of others. Strengthening your AIC through MindSET brain exercises, allows you to tune into your own sense of empathy to increase your ability to know what others are feeling.

The brain contains neurons that have mirror properties. This means that these neurons activate in your brain when someone *else* is doing something. If you watch a person take a bite of soufflé, your brain activates as though you took a bite of soufflé. These neurons are called *mirror neurons*, but that is a bit of a misnomer. There aren't just a few special neurons that have this property. It seems like lots of neurons have this capability. In one study, 25% of the neurons that were observed had the ability to activate when someone else was doing a particular action. It might be that a lot of our neurons are able to activate just by watching someone else do something.

When you see another person close their finger in a door, you know it hurts. More than just *know* it hurts, you experience the result of the pain in your body as though you closed your own finger in the door. You can't feel the pain in your hand, but your body gets sensations as though you could feel it. You might wince, have an adrenaline spike, feel sweaty or faint, and all because someone else got hurt. You experience the brain activity associated with pain. You experience the emotions that the other person has along with their pain.

## Exercise: Emotion Calibration and Empathy

*Record your response for audio or video journaling.*

You can learn a lot about how someone else is feeling simply by understanding how you are feeling.

To begin: Sit in a comfortable and private space. Think about a hurtful conflict that you have with someone else. Imagine they are in front of you. Tell them, either in your mind or out loud, how you feel about what's going on. Don't hold back, you can't do any damage to the relationship since you are alone in private. When you feel intense emotion, stop talking and simply notice your feelings. Say what your emotions are without giving reasons. Leave out all rationalizations or because clauses.

> Like this: "I feel angry and scared. My heart is pounding."
> NOT: "I feel angry and scared <u>because</u> my heart is pounding."
> NOT: "I feel angry and scared <u>because</u> you wronged me."

Now, think about the other person. Recognize the empathy in your experience. All interactions include the same emotions on both sides. That's how emotion works. The person involved in this conflict shares the same emotional experience. In this case they are also angry and scared. They may be expressing those feelings quite differently than you are.

How this works: Emotions are shared through mirror neurons. Humans feel each other's emotions. So, if you feel a certain way, those around you feel it too, whether they are able to recognize their feelings or not.

Pitfalls: When you give reasons for emotions, the exercise becomes an exercise in rational thought and the emotional calibration cannot happen.

---

Authenticity is key to empathy. Your brain knows when someone is really in pain, and when they are faking. When you see someone pick up a coffee cup, your brain experiences what happens when you pick up a coffee cup. If they mimic the action, like pretending to pick up the cup, but not really doing it, your brain doesn't respond the same way.

Transmitting a message through the mirror neuron system is dependent on authentic expressions of actions and emotions.

Actors learn to conjure genuine emotions when they are trained using Method Acting. They can portray authentic feelings to the audience. They do this by remembering past experiences that were associated with the emotion they want to convey. The goal is for the actor to authentically feel the emotion which then, transmits the emotion to the audience through their mirror system. The mirror system in each audience member's brain activates when the emotion is authentic and doesn't activate when emotion is faked.

What do you think happens if you fake an emotion to cover another emotion, like when you put on a happy face even though you feel angry? It's likely that you'd confuse those around you. They will experience anger while you grin at them. They might come to think that they don't trust you or that they are angry at you for something they can't quite figure out.

Empathy is not limited to watching another person. In the lab, scientists have measured activation of neurons associated with walking, in a subject who is merely listening to someone talk about walking. When they heard someone talk about talking, neurons associated with talking activated. Simply discussing an action is enough to activate your nervous system as though you were doing it. Scientists don't know the bounds of this mirror system. It doesn't seem to be located in any one place in the brain. There is enough evidence to show that we are wired to feel each other.

## Needs and Fulfillment

Through empathy, all people can transmit joy and suffering and any other complicated set of emotions to any other person who will focus long enough to receive the message. There is a very strong web of connection that binds us together. If you saw yourself as connected to all the people in the world, how could you possibly get lonely?

Many people tend to cut themselves off from using empathy and, in turn, create loneliness for themselves. Those who have not calibrated their emotional pain thresholds cannot bear to feel the emotions of others. It's too painful. And so develops a self-inflicted life of separateness, starting with a severing of intimate connections to others.

Separateness is a big deal. Loss, loneliness, needs, desires all rely on separateness. Suffering relies on attachment according to Buddhist philosophy. This word, *attachment*, has lost some meaning in translation. It's not the attachment that creates suffering, it's the belief that you are separate from the thing you wish to be attached to. Thus, it's really the separateness that causes suffering.

You can be attached to an idea, object, or person like a child is attached to a teddy bear. When the bear is close by, all is well. When the bear is out of sight, suffering occurs. Proximity of the bear matters only when the child sees the bear as separate from himself. But what counts as *separate*? If the bear is out of sight, is that separateness? If the bear is on the floor and the child is on the bed, is that separateness? Each child will define his own idea of separateness. The child creates conditions under which everything is ok and conditions under which things are not ok. Conditions aren't based in any law of nature, they are simply beliefs that the child has constructed to avoid suffering. These belief constructs are superstitions.[12]

Highly regarded child psychologist Jean Piaget identified a similar concept that he called *object permanence*. At some point in a child's development, the child learns that an object continues to exist when it is hidden from view. With very young children, you can put a toy in a box and the child doesn't seek the toy anymore. It seems as though "out of sight, out of mind" applies to very young children. Older children will behave in a way that makes it clear they know the toy still exists. You can put a toy in a box and the child will open the box to find the toy. Learning that an object exists even when out of view is considered a normal part of childhood development.

---

[12] Even birds are superstitious. Pigeons in a cage with levers and buttons to press in order to receive food will make up a pattern that they will repeat. Even when they are fed randomly, they will keep repeating the pattern that worked most often for them.

**Exercise: Human Needs**

Many of the things that people need to be happy are non-tangible, which means it's hard to be sure whether those needs have been met.

To begin: Look at Maslow's list of human needs and make an argument about how you are connected to the fulfillment of each human need.

- Physiological needs like food, shelter, water.
- Safety needs like personal safety and the safety of loved ones.
- Connection to others like intimacy, friendship, and family.
- Ability to see one's self as valid through self-respect and confidence.

Why this works: Since many human needs are intangible, it's often not clear whether you are in need or fulfilled. When you can show your brain that you have fulfillment, then it can rest assured that all is well.

Pitfalls: Don't worry about showing a lot of evidence. Even the simplest argument is enough to satisfy your brain.

Buddhist philosophy takes this idea of object permanence a step farther. This advanced developmental notion is that the object itself isn't important. It's the benefit that the object conveys that is important. Teddy bears bring joy and comfort, that is the benefit of a teddy bear. Like an object that still exists even when it's hidden in a box, the benefit of the object is still available when the object itself isn't available. For now, we'll call this *benefit permanence*. A teddy bear can bring joy and comfort even when it is in another room, out of sight. Another example comes from a classic Disney film Dumbo. Dumbo's feather is an enchanted object that allowed the elephant to fly. When the feather is lost, Dumbo learns that he doesn't need the feather to fly. He could fly all along and the feather was simply an object that reminded him of that benefit.

In Buddhism, benefit permanence translates to non-attachment. The benefits that are conveyed from an object exist even when the object is not present. Those who are able to find the wisdom in non-attachment feel connected to everything in a way that doesn't allow for the object to be removed from them, no matter how far away that object goes. If you haven't come to this wisdom yet, you might find this to be really hard to understand. How can a person feel connected to every object on the planet? It might seem far fetched, but you've likely already come to this understanding on some level in your own way. Think about your own childhood teddy bear, blanket, or object of attachment. You probably haven't seen it in a long time, if it exists anymore, and yet, you still feel that object in your heart. This ability to know that you have the positive feelings and other benefits of your teddy bear with you always is similar to non-attachment.

Sometimes people agree on the things in life that are hard, and other times we don't. The hard parts of life, the parts that we might include under the descriptor of *suffering* are not always the same for everyone. You may have seen this disconnect when some events cause suffering for some but not for others. A simple family road trip can highlight this variation in experience between individuals. One sibling seems to suffer and the rest of the family can't figure out how to help them. Then empathy kicks in and the whole family begins to suffer together. Under the same conditions, why do some people suffer while others are content? Why isn't suffering universal?

Suffering is different for everyone because everyone has their own pain thresholds and their own belief constructs. Children will naturally come up with their own beliefs about needs from their teddy bears. One kid will cry when the bear is two feet away. Another will let his bear leave the room without incident. The delineation between what causes joy and what causes suffering is specific to individual children. This variation is the same with adults. Adults create belief constructs about attachments to things in their lives too. Events that cause suffering will be different between adults. Childhood attachments are easy to see: teddy bears, blankets, parents, siblings, a favorite bottle or plate. Adult attachments, like adults themselves, are rather complicated but the basic premise is the same. People invent ideas about what's ok and what's a cause for concern. Another way to say this is that people invent beliefs about their own needs. When they do, those needs become as real as a teddy bear.

Abraham Maslow, a psychologist who studied very successful people, is known for creating the hierarchy of human needs. He is called the father of humanistic psychology because he was one of the first to study people who weren't suffering. Prior to his work, psychology was a study of mental illness and abnormal behavior. He was well-connected in his field; his mentor Alfred Adler learned psychology from Sigmund Freud. Although Freud has many critics, he was responsible for pushing the field of psychology into talk therapy. Prior to that time, mental illness was treated physically with surgery or other manipulations of the brain, likely resulting in unnecessary brain damage for many patients.

Maslow's *hierarchy of needs* is taught in business schools as a way for students to understand what motivates employees. Maslow's work found its way into business pedagogy through his management book, *Maslow on Management*, and his work has been cited over and over as the doctrine of human motivation in since the 1960s. Maslow painstakingly itemized all of the things that people tend to say that they need. He basically created the list of things that have the potential to cause suffering if not fulfilled. It's called a hierarchy because Maslow created an order for the needs that seemed to be more important than others and shaped it into a pyramid. The base needs are things like food, shelter, and water, then the next few layers of the pyramid include health, family, self esteem, social standing, and respect. At the very top is the need to express one's self creatively and find meaning in one's life - a part of life that he called *self actualization*. He assumed that if you didn't have food shelter and water, you would need those things before you needed to self-actualize.

The hierarchy of needs has many critics. It's certainly not a definitive understanding of human motivation. You can find lots of examples of people who express themselves creatively or seek purpose without having secured permanent access to food, shelter, and water first. Look at any professional dance troupe or professional artist community. Many self-actualized people don't have all the other tiers of the pyramid secured. The opposite is also true. You can find people who have managed to secure the lower tier needs and never bother to self-actualize. They keep their lives focused on maintaining all of their needs on the lower tiers.

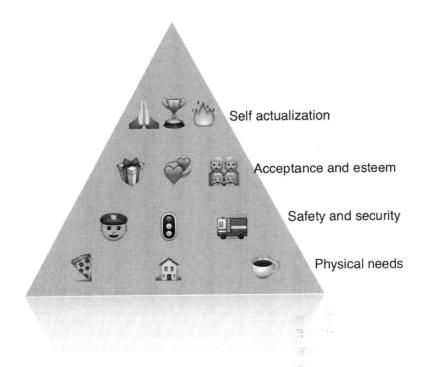

Fig. 4 – Maslow's hierarchy of needs. The basic human needs like food, shelter, and water are on the bottom tier. The top tier includes higher-level needs like creativity and religion.

Most people, and Maslow himself, would tell you that the path to happiness comes from attaining all the things on the list of needs. If that were true, happiness would be guaranteed when you have access to all the things that fulfill those human needs. But it's just not true. You can have fulfilled all basic needs and be unhappy. Fulfilling needs and happiness are not related. Instead of looking at Maslow's hierarchy of needs as a pathway to happiness, we can use it as a list of things that people tend to reference as reasons for their own suffering.

The lowest tier of Maslow's hierarchy serve to maintain the physical body. Without shelter, food, or water, the human body doesn't last very long. Assuming that the minimal requirements for the survival of the human body are taken care of, the rest of Maslow's needs are about maintaining the psyche, or the non-physical parts of a human.

You can assume that all people would benefit from having access to all of the things listed on Maslow's list but what does it really mean to have access to these things? What does it mean to have self-respect? Who is responsible for maintaining intimacy and a connection to others? When someone is suffering because they don't have self-respect, where do they turn to remedy that problem?

Some needs seem easy to fulfill alone, and other needs seem to require an accomplice to fulfill them. Solving a problem of food, water, or shelter is something you can do without assistance. When you are hungry, you find food. Either you buy some food, beg some food, or find cast off food in the trash. Other people can help you, but it isn't necessary to involve another person in the solution. When you are suffering from a lack of intimacy, how do you feed that need? At first blush, it seems like another person is required to help you in that solution. Intimacy is a close connection to another person, therefore another person must participate. Right?

The fallacy of human needs is that another person must participate in fulfilling the need. A person needing intimacy wanders around looking for another person to fill that need. They quickly discover that it's very hard to get another person to fulfill their need of intimacy for various reasons. It might be hard to get other people to spend time with them. Maybe it's hard for them to get close to others. Or finally, and most depressingly, even when they get close to another person, the need for intimacy still isn't fulfilled. This kind of need isn't something that can be fulfilled by another person.

Intimacy, and the rest of the psychological human needs are fulfilled in the same way that the adult can benefit from his teddy bear decades after it was physically lost. A person who has embraced the benefit permanence of intimacy, or in other words, is not feeling separate from intimacy, will easily find other people to be intimate with. The mental benefit of intimacy must precede the physical expression of it. Those who have positioned themselves as separate from intimacy will not be able to fulfill that need.

Designing your life with your mind may seem like a supernatural power. Think your way to more love and happiness! But there's nothing supernatural about it. Without realizing it, those who have unfulfilled needs have been holding the things that they want at bay. The way to allow those things to be fulfilled is to simply stop seeing them as separate. Dumbo's feather went missing, but he could fly anyway. The teddy bear may or may not be in your grandmother's attic, but you can still fall asleep in peace. All of the needs listed on Maslow's hierarchy are already available to you if you are willing to simply accept them. It's ok. You already have everything you need.

# Summary of Key Concepts

- Everyone's view of the world is different because we all have different beliefs that we hold to be true. Changing a belief will change your view.

- You can connect to anyone using empathy. You don't even have to speak.

- The ACC tells you to *Do something!* but you can choose to notice it and do nothing.

- You can change your sensitivity to pain and irritation by calibrating your thresholds. Different thresholds is one of the reasons that everyone has different sensitivity levels to pain and irritation.

- You can start to notice when you run around like a headless chicken. There's no need to do anything different at first. Noticing is a very big step.

- When you view yourself as separate from your human needs, you will suffer. To feel better, notice how you are not separate from those things.

# 3: Perspective Shift

*The only true voyage of discovery... is to possess other eyes, to behold the universe through the eyes of another, of a hundred others, to behold the hundred universes that each of them beholds.*

Marcel Proust, The Prisoner

Maslow, the psychologist we met at the end of the last chapter, studied people who were at the top of their fields. That's how he pulled together the hierarchy of needs and many of his other contributions to psychology. By many accounts, however, Maslow himself was a miserable person. He was able to see how the successful people he studied were capable of fulfilling their own needs, but he wasn't able to crack the code for himself. Maslow wrote openly about hating his mother, who he made out to be a monstrous person with mental illness. His many siblings, however, didn't feel the same way about their mother. They were hurt by his suggestions that she was anything other than an average loving mother. Maslow was also convinced that his face was deformed and that he scared people on the public bus with his looks. Maslow was an average looking person, not frightening at all, and his siblings all claim that they had a normal childhood. Why was Maslow's experience so different from theirs?

What Maslow missed was that two people can have exactly the same life, same income, same household, same diet, same work, same friends, and if one sees himself as separate from anything that he desires, he will suffer. Maslow thought the magic was in having the needs fulfilled, but he didn't realize that *fulfilled* was a code word for *not separate*.

Things are not what they seem to be. The world looks like it's made up of people with strengths and weaknesses. Haves and have nots. Friends and enemies. The world looks as though it follows rules and we learn those rules to navigate the world. The joke's on us. The human brain is devoted to identifying patterns. We see them everywhere. Every bit of new information we encounter is compared to the closest memories. When something remotely matches, we believe that we understand it implicitly. Maslow believed he understood how people on the city bus saw him. He believed that he was mistreated by a terrible mother. Things were not what they seemed to be for Maslow.

Some people are able to see through the illusion that their ideas of the world match the world implicitly. And rest assured, it is an illusion. The human brain creates this illusion as a trick of pattern recognition. The world is however you believe it to be. If you believe you have something, you do. If you believe you are lacking something, you are. The idea of, "Believe it and it's real" is the theme of countless children's movies, so the notion might seem a bit childish or fantastical but it's based in neuroscience. Your brain is an expert at pattern recognition and you will find evidence to support whatever you believe.

What happens then, if you believe nothing? If by some magic or strength of mind, you were able to clear all of your beliefs about the world, how might the world look to you? You wouldn't be so busy fitting the world into your patterns of belief. Instead, you would have the freedom of mind to observe, without judgment or patterns, whatever you see before you. To truly see the world as it is, all preconceived beliefs must vanish.

It's possible, but very difficult, to remove all of your beliefs, so that isn't going to be the goal you set for yourself, dear reader. Might there be another way to see things as they are, not as they seem to be? You can learn to practice the art of perspective shift. You can do this right now. Look at any object, then walk around to another side, and then another. When your mind understands this object from many angles, it's less likely to jump to conclusions about one pattern. It's easier to step back from your beliefs about the world and see them as illusions when you aren't strongly attached to one version of reality.

**Exercise: Perspective Shift 1**

To begin: You'll need a smartphone or camera.

1.  Choose an object to study, preferably one larger than your fist. If it's movable, place it on a table where you can walk around it. If it's very large, it's best if you can walk around the object.
2.  Take a photo of the object from the side (not from above) so that there is background in the photo.
3.  Walk around the object and take two more photos from different directions.
4.  Now compare the photos.

How is the object different when you look at it from different sides? How is the background context different in the different photos? How does the background influence the way the object looks? If you gave one of these pictures to one person and another of these pictures to a different person, how might their ideas of the object and backgrounds differ?

Why this works: When you look at a picture of an object, it's clear that different perspectives will give you different information about the same object. It's harder to understand that phenomenon when you are discussing politics, relationships, or acceptable behavior.

Pitfalls: Be careful not to include judgments about perspectives. The point is that things look different depending on where you stand.

Successful people know that they can use their ability to shift perspective to get whatever they want. In countless college graduation speeches and political campaigns orators repeat, "You can do anything you want as long as you are willing to work for it." Unfortunately, the secret is lost in that sentence. Those who already know what it means will nod along. Those who haven't discovered the meaning will ask themselves just *how hard* do I have to work? I'm trying!

Getting what you want is not about working hard, it's about shifting perspective to find a way. Maslow didn't have to work hard to have a life where he was at peace on the city bus instead of worrying that he was terrifying commuters with his looks. His suffering came from his own imagination and his own illusion of what others thought of him. What might have happened if Maslow could've shifted his perspective to see himself from an outsider's point of view? It would have been a perspective that didn't include the painful emotions that made him believe that he was so frighteningly ugly. He'd have seen himself sitting with strangers who didn't care at all what he looked like. The only terrified person on that bus was him.

Successful people have figured out that they are not separate from the things they want. When you believe you are separate from what you want, you will find evidence to support that belief. Separateness causes suffering. All people suffer when they feel separate. A child suffers when he feels separate from his teddy bear. An adult suffers when he feels separate from safety, money, love, a nice car, a better job, self-respect, a sense of purpose, or anything else on Maslow's hierarchy of needs. What is the simple difference between those who succeed and those who suffer? Those who succeed can work out the path between themselves and their desires. Those who suffer see themselves as separate from their desires.

To want something assumes that you don't yet have it. But there are two ways to see something you don't yet have. Successful people can see their object of desire as distanced from them and strategic effort is the only thing standing in the way of achieving it. They work to shift their perspective to find the paths that connect them to what they want. Then, they are willing to do what it takes to follow the path to get there. This is what people mean by being "willing to work for it." First you identify the object of desire and notice that you are simply distanced from it. Then you map out the path to get there and work the path. Being distanced from something does not cause suffering. Instead it causes motivation to stir deep inside.

Mapping out the path between your current life and the life you want is key to your ability to achieve it. You may be making a modest salary and you want to double it. You can successfully increase your salary. First, you must use perspective shift to see your career and money-making potential from many angles. How do you see your potential? How does your closest friend see your potential? How does your mentor see your potential? Next, you need to remove beliefs that block your ability to see how an increase in income is possible. You will learn more about removing beliefs in later chapters. Uninhibited by beliefs and able to see your life from many angles, you will find a path to make twice as much money as you are making now. Then you have to decide if you have the appetite to go forward on that path.

What does it mean to have the appetite to go forward? Most people see themselves as separate from their objects of desire. Being separate from an object and being distanced from an object might seem like a semantic difference, but it's not. Understanding the nuance between these two perspectives will allow you to suffer less, so it's a fundamental concept. Being distanced from an object means that there's work to do in order to reach it. Telling yourself that you can have pizza for lunch if you are willing to walk ten blocks allows your mind to do the math. Do I want pizza so badly that I'll walk ten blocks? Telling yourself that you can't have pizza is a different experience altogether. The experience of the word *can't* is the equivalent of separation and therefore creates suffering.

Anyone can make the leap from separateness to distance. It's a perspective shift. It costs nothing and requires no education. It requires no action. You can do it from your couch, from the front seat of your car, or from your office chair. All it requires is for you to stop fighting for separateness. When you do this, you will be infinitely closer to the things you desire.

The people in this chapter have discovered that they are not separate from the things that they want. Instead, they see themselves as distanced from the things that they want. They create paths in their minds to determine just how many figurative blocks they will have to walk to get there. When a desire is difficult to attain, they ask themselves whether they have the appetite to do that much work. The path to any desire is no different than walking a distance for pizza. When the distance is larger than their appetite, they choose not to move forward. When the appetite out measures the distance, they go for it. Successful people know that they can have anything they want, as long as they are willing to work for it.

**Exercise: Perspective Shift 2**

Find a willing partner for this exercise.

To begin: Ask a friend to tell you something with which they expect you to disagree. It can be political, religious, fashion oriented, or any topic as long as you naturally tend to disagree with your friend.

Listen to them talk about this topic without responding. You say nothing. Use perspective shift to mentally see their point from multiple angles. How might you think about this if you were in your friend's shoes. How might you see this point if you were someone else entirely? Notice your own emotions and your body. Are you tense, relaxed, sad, angry?

In this exercise, you don't agree, disagree, believe or disbelieve. You listen and seek multiple perspectives. Perform no further actions. When the exercise is over, do not follow up to share your opinion. Let it go. Not making judgments and not performing actions is a very important part of this exercise.

Why it works: When we listen, we tend to anchor what we hear to the information we already know. When listening to perspectives that we don't agree with, there is a strong urge to somehow fit the information into what we know. Noticing that urge and doing nothing is a powerful way to begin listening to new perspectives without an agenda.

Pitfall: You may find that you judge your friend's perspectives. If this happens, notice that judgment and do nothing. You can calibrate your urge to make judgments too!

# Appetite for Success

Tom Higley, a serial entrepreneur, is now regarded as a success, but if you'd met him when he was 17, you'd have never predicted that he'd become a multimillionaire. He barely passed his classes in high school and he admits that it was his English teacher who pulled some strings to make sure he officially graduated. Tom's inauspicious start aside, he practiced a few skills that have made all the difference in his life. Tom is able to see that he is distanced from what he wants, not separate. He uses the art of perspective shift to help him see the path to his desires. His ability to figure out if he has the appetite to go the distance has allowed him to do things few others have accomplished. Tom knows that his only limitation is his willingness.

When you meet Tom, you can tell there's something special about him. He's smart and charismatic. His grey eyes are piercing and intense. You can't help but listen to him; the enthusiasm behind his words is infectious. Tom can also read minds. Of course, I don't mean this literally. Since Tom's mind is not clouded with conflicts, he's able to listen so well that he can hear the deep meaning in people's words. The ability to listen is another secret to his success. Imagine how much easier it is to negotiate with someone when they've already told you all their secrets. In fact, people tell their secrets all the time, all you have to do is listen like Tom does.

Tom is human. He's not perfect. He's often late. He's self-deprecating. Sometimes he dresses as though he pulled his clothes out of the hamper. Tom doesn't have magical powers. He is capable of shouting, getting angry, and being in reaction, but those behaviors are rare occurrences. Tom's success is quite simple. He chooses his goals based on his appetite for the effort it takes to achieve those goals. And, he deeply listens to people as he works with them to achieve those goals.

The things that make Tom successful are skills that you can learn too. Actually, you already have those skills, you just don't know it. You have beliefs blocking the way. By the time you are done reading this book, you will likely have found at least one belief that is causing you conflicts. After you learn how to retire the first belief, it's just a matter of time and willingness to keep hunting for more beliefs. Eventually, your mind can be clear of conflicts. You'd be surprised how those beliefs keep you from listening to what people are really telling you. Beliefs allow you to hold tight to the illusion that you are separate from what you want. When you clear your mind of these distractions, you will notice more opportunities for things you might have the appetite to accomplish.

Tom's life includes seemingly large leaps from one kind of life to another. He took a unique path from a high school near-dropout to a multimillionaire. No one could have predicted how his life would go. When you know that your only limitation is your appetite, you can make jumps from one career to another. You can prove naysayers wrong. Nothing can stop you. Tom's story is a testament to the power of an unpredictable life.

Tom wasn't a good student in high school because he was too busy playing his guitar. Shortly after high school, he became a lead guitarist for the DeBarge Family, an R&B band from Michigan that is still actively playing at the time of this writing. The night Tom found himself opening for Barry White and the Love Limited Orchestra is his favorite memory from those days. Now decades later, Tom says that he's glad he didn't stay in professional music. Many of the DeBarge Family band members ended up in jail or dead from overdoses. It was a hard life. Tom saw musical success early, but he also knew that being a musician would make for a challenging family life. He wanted to get married and have a family. He also wanted to be able to provide for his family so he decided to become a lawyer. To do that, he had to go back to school.

While he was in the music world, Tom was distanced from a college education. He didn't hang out with the college folks and his academic track record was terrible. On the surface, it might have looked impossible for Tom to get into college, let alone finish college. It looked like he was a long way away from college success, but Tom knew better. He understood that his own success was about his appetite, not his track record. Tom also knew that his appetite was invisible to others. No one would believe that he had an appetite to complete college until he showed some academic success. It took a few semesters at the local community college for Tom to prove to the admissions committee of a four-year university that he was serious about school. He graduated from the University of Michigan and went on to get his Juris Doctor degree from Harvard Law school. Tom's appetite to become a lawyer allowed him to settle down with his new wife and start a family on solid financial footing.

I bet you can think of many different beliefs that might have prevented Tom from getting into Harvard Law. He might have believed that he didn't have the academic track record to get accepted. He might have believed that risking a rejection from Harvard Law would hurt him. He might have believed that he wasn't the right kind of person to work in law. There are infinite ways that Tom could have sabotaged his own success with a belief that limited him.

Tom used his appetite as a decision-making guide. He had not done well in high school, but that lack of success didn't deter him. He knew that his current appetite was more important than his past track record. When Tom showed up in class on his first day at Harvard Law, he had no evidence that he'd pass his classes or graduate. His future was uncertain and he pushed through anyway. His decision to pick a top-tier law school was the first in a series of decisions that Tom made in spite of a lack of evidence for his future success.

Tom became a fine attorney and his growing family relished the stable income that he got from that job. However, six years into his law career, Tom decided to quit. He left a comfortable career to start an internet-based company. This was another audacious move for Tom. He had never run a company before and had no evidence that he'd be any good at being a CEO. Also, the company he chose to start was an internet company during the early years of the internet; it was focused on a technology that had not been recognized as the fundamental technology that we know it to be today.

What was he after? Why would someone with small children leave a good job to dive into an uncharted world of internet companies? He was driven by his own interest for computers and the internet. He had purchased a Macintosh computer in 1984, the first year they were available, and he saw what the future would hold. Tom saw how personal computers could replace the secretaries in his law firm. It was clear to him that instead of lawyers having a personal secretary to beautifully type their letters and notes, he predicted that lawyers would have a personal computer to type their own notes. Whereas another person might have seen the dying analog world of typewriters and mimeographs, Tom saw the bright new future of computers and digital files. His goal was to stay relevant in a changing world and he had the appetite to lead the way into new information technology.

The company Tom started was called NETdelivery Corporation and he launched it in 1995, well before the internet was being used by everyone. To give you an idea of just how early this company was, it held the patent on the (now very basic) technology to put a hyperlink in an email. Tom had absolutely no evidence that everyone would be devoted to email just a few years later. Tom had no evidence that the internet would become the game changer that it did or that his company would make money, but he knew he had the appetite to give it his full attention.

Again, beliefs could have limited Tom's decisions. He might have believed that he was risking his family's future by leaving the law firm. He might have believed that his wife would be angry with him if he followed his interests. He might have believed that he was too old to change careers. Fortunately for him, he knew that his appetite was all that mattered.

Making decisions based on your appetite works when you have the integrity to stay true to your appetite. Take the simple example of walking ten blocks to get pizza. You might find that your shoes cause a blister; a sidewalk is closed; it's raining; or it's very hot outside. Conditions change and you can't predict what you will have to overcome to get this pizza. Walking ten blocks might be easy or it might be miserable. What will you do if you walk halfway, and then conditions change? Will you turn around, soldier on, or change course?
Imagine a person so dedicated to getting that they will do anything. They return to their office, feet bloody from blisters, clothes torn from being chased by street dogs, sweaty, tired, and injured, but with pizza in hand. Is this success? Or is this an obsession with pizza?

Imagine another person who returns back to their office empty-handed. They walked the whole way and realized at the counter that their wallet was back in the office. Is this true willingness? Or is this self-sabotage?

Imagine a third person who got pizza. They had to walk 16 blocks because a few streets were closed for repairs. They discovered this change in plans midway in the journey. They made a new assessment. Is pizza worth a 16 block walk? They determined that yes, they are willing to walk 16 blocks for pizza, and kept going. A twenty block walk would have been a different story.

Tom doesn't blindly adhere to his goals. Everyday he shifts his perspective and focus to look at things as they are. This is similar to the way that the last person shifted their self-inquiry about pizza. Making decisions based on appetite is something you do continuously. You keep updating your perspective, especially in light of new information. You have to be self-aware for your appetite to be your driver. Each day, you have to assess the situation afresh. In light of today's information, do you still have the appetite to go on? You have to listen to your internal willingness and not listen to the incessant chatter of beliefs about what *should* be happening.

Building NETdelivery didn't feel like a success to Tom. He was able to raise $1.5M from venture capitalists, but the investors were not satisfied with his leadership or his vision for the company. In the end, he was fired from the company he founded and left feeling as though he failed. Did Tom fail?

Tom's relationship with NETdelivery didn't go as he wanted. Certainly, he didn't set out to build a company just to be ousted by his own investors. However, against all lack of evidence, the professional musician turned lawyer was able to build a company which put him in a position to connect with more opportunities in the future. When he left NETdelivery Corporation, he retired briefly to focus on music again. He decided to write a musical that he called *Startup*. His creative work was cathartic.

# Rising from the Ashes

NETdelivery might not have been the direct success that Tom hoped it would be, however, the work that he put into his first company did eventually pay off. While Tom worked on his musical, a new opportunity began to quietly develop out of the relationships he had made while working on NETdelivery.

While Tom was raising money, he met a lot of people. One of those people was Brad Feld, who is now a remarkably successful venture capitalist and entrepreneurship advocate. Brad became an advisor to NETdelivery and through that relationship Tom and Brad were able to get to know each other well.

By 1997 Brad was a venture capitalist at SoftBank, and he was working to pull together a team that could build a new internet company. Some of the legwork necessary to start a company was already underway when

Brad contacted Tom to see if he'd be willing to participate. Although Tom had set out to write his musical, he reassessed his goal in light of new information. Brad's offer was another chance for Tom to run an internet-based business. After a lot of research into the new business opportunity, and some time to get to know the other people who were slated to be involved, Tom no longer had an appetite for writing a musical. He was ready to be a CEO again.

Building a company is hard work and many companies fail. Tom could have looked at his failure with NETdelivery and decided that he wasn't going to press his luck a second time. He could have assumed that he wasn't cut out to be a CEO when he was fired from his first company. Tom didn't think like that. He had the appetite to do it again so, he got to work. Tom and the rest of the team quickly built Service Metrics and sold it 18 months later to another company called Exodus. Twenty-seven of the sixty-eight employees of Service Metrics became millionaires in January of 2000 when the company sold.

Service Metrics was a huge win for Tom, for his employees, and for the venture capitalists that invested in the company, but it almost didn't work out that way. When the company first launched, Tom and his cofounders were able to raise $1M and they used the next six months to build a very successful software as a service (SaaS) product. He got a phone call from a potential customer who loved the service and wanted to hire Service Metrics to build custom metrics software for their exclusive use. Although they had offered a large sum of money that would increase the revenue that Service Metrics was generating, Tom turned down the work.

Imagine you are a cofounder working in a company that is struggling to grow quickly and your CEO turns down a significant amount of revenue. You might be horrified. They had the $1M investment, and some early revenue, but Tom had not raised the second round of investment that the company would need to execute on the strategic plan. The company was inching toward success, but it wasn't there yet.

Tom did succeed in raising another funding round; he closed $14.5M in investment in that second round. The company took off. They were hiring like crazy and they saw extraordinary growth. The company didn't suffer after Tom so brazenly turned down a significant revenue stream.

But why did he do it? Why didn't he just do the custom work and take in the revenue.

Exodus was a prospective customer when they asked Service Metrics to make custom software just for them and they would pay enough for it that Service Metrics could keep increasing revenue. On the surface, this seems like it would have been a good decision. But Tom knew this wasn't as simple as it looked. They didn't have the resources to run their primary company and to do custom software work for a client. They had to choose. Either become a custom software company, or continue on the path of building their SaaS product and trying to raise the second round of funding.

What you may not be considering here is that Tom had made some agreements that he needed to uphold. When Tom took $1M in equity investment from venture capitalists, he made an agreement to do his best to return their investment back to them, along with additional money as a return on their investment. The only way to uphold that agreement was to ignore the offer for custom software work and continue on the path they were on. If they took the custom software option, they would never return money to the investors.

For Tom, this was a no-brainer. He made his decisions based on his appetite and his ability to uphold the integrity of his agreements. Tom made agreements with investors that he would do his best to get them a return on investment. So, Tom turned down the custom software work. The company flourished under his leadership. It benefitted from his focused direction. Only half a year after raising the second round, Tom had gathered multiple viable offers to purchase Service Metrics. He started planning how he was going to sell the company and return money to investors.

Exodus initially made an offer of $79M to buy Service Metrics. Tom's company had seen incredible growth in a short time and Tom had amassed other offers. He was well positioned to negotiate a bigger price tag so he turned down their offer. Remember, Exodus was the same company that wanted to use Service Metrics as a custom software shop and Tom turned them down for that too. However, the folks at Exodus weren't daunted by Tom's negotiation tactics and they wanted the software solution that Service Metrics offered.

How did Tom have multiple offers to buy Service Metrics? Was he just lucky? He was listening. Tom was in the middle of negotiating a large, long-term service contract with a prospective customer and he discovered that they were considering buying Service Metrics instead of executing a purchase contract. He knew that he would get a better deal if he had two or more viable choices when it came time to sell the company. Tom had the appetite to see how many potential acquisition partners he could gather in a short time frame. He was able to secure five viable options which put him and the company in a very good position to negotiate.

Service Metrics sold to Exodus for $280M. Additionally, as chance would have it, Exodus stock rose dramatically after the transaction. No one could sell their shares until a few months passed because of some agreements that were put in place to protect stockholders from volatility after acquisition. When they were able to turn their stock back into cash, the total price tag on Service Metrics was $1.1B. Tom, the investors, and Service Metrics employees all did very well.

How did Tom make such an extraordinary comeback after getting fired from his first venture capital-backed company? Tom might have been nervous about making decisions at Service Metrics after having been fired by his investors at NETdelivery. Tom knew that failure was always a possibility, but he'd learned a lot from his experience at NETdelivery and he knew that he had the appetite to run another company. Sure, he could have failed again, but that's not the way it happened.

When Service Metrics got the initial request from Exodus to perform custom software work, the company was running low on cash. Tom could have panicked and allowed his ACC to tell him to run around like a chicken with his head cut off. Instead, Tom didn't change course. He didn't take on the new work that would have distracted his team from their strategic plan. He continued his fundraising efforts and had the software team continue making the product that they had set out to make. If Tom had let his ACC run the show, the outcome might have been very different.

# Your Role in the Larger Play

Remember Michael and Susan Simpson, the couple who lived in Russia? Susan was officially coaching and teaching through a multinational organization. And Michael? Well, he was not. Michael became deeply involved with Susan's work, but he didn't have an official position for his first couple of years in Russia. During that time Michael was just hanging out, trying to make himself useful where he could. He had previous experience doing business in the US where corporate ethics are strong, and he was a certified executive coach. Although he didn't have the right documentation to work in Russia, he was certainly qualified to support professional development.

The men in the office wanted to learn life skills from Michael. When the Russian men saw the respectful relationship that Michael and Susan shared, they started to get curious about how respectful relationship dynamics were possible. In Russia at the time, it was common for husbands and wives to have contentious relationships. A few men approached Michael to see if they could understand what Michael was doing to earn Susan's respect and affection.

Family relationships, like most relationships in Russia at that time, were full of conflict. Michael said it was common to see mothers berating their male children on the playground. Their shouts were not focused on common childhood foibles like forgetting a coat or getting dirty. On more than one occasion he heard mothers tell their sons, "You'll never amount to anything, just like your father." Interpersonal conflict in Russia was the cultural norm. The Russian men who worked alongside Susan in the ministry had lived their whole lives without positive role models. Conflict was pervasive.

When you live in the midst of anger and conflict, it's hard to see how you can possibly do anything to change it. It feels like the conflict comes from the outside; it seems to come from the other people in your life. Often, those around you seem to be obviously at fault for the conflict. However, they act as though you are at fault. Who is right?

No matter how confusing and irreparable a conflict seems to be, it can be solved if one person is willing to solve it. This story was set in Russia, in a historic time of extreme violence and conflict. Relationships between men and women were tense nationwide. There was a culture of conflict in many, if not most, households. Yet, individual relationships were repaired when one of the people in the household became willing to do what was necessary to end the conflict.

Michael was able to help Susan's Russian colleagues see the patterns that had formed in their relationships. He saw how many of the women in Russia were unhappy with their lives and how they often pushed their husbands away. Before meeting Michael, the Russian men went into reaction when their wives pushed them away. Michael was able to help the men see things from a new perspective and it made all the difference.

The true change in a conflict comes from a perspective shift and it only takes one person to make that shift. Michael helped the Russian men see that they could choose to behave differently in their relationships. Instead of going into reaction when their wives pushed them away, the men were able to choose to respond to their wives with acceptance, patience, and kindness.

It's easy to go into reaction yourself when you are confronted with a person who is already in reaction. When you are focused on a person who is experiencing intense emotions, you will feel those emotions through your sense of empathy. You might even find logical arguments to defend your right to go into reaction. I've heard this argument, "I can't just sit back let them talk badly to me like that." Basically, you have two choices when you are in a conflict, either let that conflict persist, or take the responsibility to begin the process of ending the conflict.

To end a conflict, you will have to a play a new role. You can't simply behave in the way you always have behaved in the conflict, or the conflict will continue as it has in the past. Changing your behavior is much easier if you start with a change in your perspective. A true perspective shift will naturally influence a true behavior change. Feeling compassion for someone who is suffering allows you to see through the details of their unpleasant behavior. They might be aggressive, aloof, or exhibiting any combination of uninviting behaviors. It's difficult to be around someone who is suffering. Finding a perspective that includes compassion makes it easier.

We underestimate the power that a single person's perspective can have on a conflict. Even when conflict is cultural like in the story above, one person's shift in perspective can end the conflict permanently. Cultural conflict happens in families, in offices, and in other types of communities. Often we feel like it doesn't matter what we do, because there are other people involved and they aren't working toward improving the culture. Fortunately, when you choose to solve a conflict, you don't need the rest of the community to help. No one has to know that you are making a change. Your perspective shift will create ripples of behavior change starting with you.

---

**Exercise: Perspective Shift 3**

Record your response for audio or video journaling, or write this as a letter.

To begin: Sit in a comfortable and private space. Choose a conflict that you have had with another person, alive or dead. Pretend that person is in the room and tell them your side of the conflict. Don't hold back; this is an exercise for you. When you have explained yourself completely, your side is done. Now, you will pretend to be the other person. Respond as they would to the accusations or explanations you just gave.

When you look at the other person's side how do you feel? How did your perspective about the reality of the situation change?

Why this works: Your brain is wired to make a solid argument for whatever position you've chosen. When you are forced to argue both sides, you see how easy it is to find good arguments for the opposing position. It's hard to feel righteous after having argued both sides.

Pitfalls: The goal of this exercise is not to solve the problem. Don't bother doing that now. The goal is simply to be able to see two sides of a conflict.

---

# Changing Relationship Dynamics

Conflict happens everywhere, but you can manage conflict no matter the source. Many people are familiar with conflict at work or at home. It can feel unmanageable, larger than yourself, and impossible to control. Fortunately, just like the Russian men who were fighting against generations of cultural strife, it only takes one perspective shift to make a huge change in a relationship. Once you get good at the skill of shifting your perspective, then you will be able to do it every time you have a conflict with someone else.

It's easy to feel hopeless about a conflict with another person. The relationship can seem as though it is hinged on the other person's behavior. You know in your heart that you want things to be different, but you can't be sure that they do too. You might find yourself asking, "How can I get *them* to be different?" Now you know how to change any relationship. Another person's behavior in your relationship is dependent on *your* perspective. If you change your perspective, their behavior cannot persist for long in light of that change.

Getting to a new perspective is the key to changing any relationship dynamic. You might be in conflict with your spouse, your coworker, a neighbor, or anyone else. If you can find a perspective in which you don't blame them for their behavior, instead you see how they are behaving in the most logical way possible given the situation, then you've found the key to ending the conflict. But how can you find a path to seeing things from their perspective?

Your spouse leaves the kitchen and bathroom in a state that drives you nuts. You think you are dealing with a lazy person who is reliant on you to manage everything in the house. Can you find a perspective that allows you to see that behavior as perfectly reasonable for the situation? When you can see their behavior, not as a weakness, but as something you'd do too if you were in their shoes, then you can talk to them in a way that will change the dynamic.

Changing your role in a relationship requires perspective shift, but to be able to make the shift, you will have to use the other skills you've learned so far. You will have to use the skill of noticing extensively. You have to notice emotions that you feel and the sensations in your body. You have to notice the intense thoughts that come into your head. Wading through all of the blame, anger, frustration, reasons, and other intense energy associated with this relationship will take a significant amount of noticing. Like an explorer slashing through the jungle with a machete, you will notice these thoughts and feelings and move through them to see what's behind them. If you are content to stop and investigate one series of thoughts, you will never find what you are looking for, which is a new perspective. Keep moving. Keep noticing. Do nothing.

Inevitably, you will find yourself going into reaction. This is inevitable because this relationship is a big problem for you. If it were a little nuisance, you probably wouldn't bother with all of this effort toward changing the relationship. You probably care a lot about this relationship and the outcome matters greatly to you. Going into reaction is a side effect of caring a lot. Unfortunately, it's not a productive state. You'll have to use your ACC calibration skills to get out of reaction in the moment so you can have productive conversations toward a new relationship dynamic.

When you are in reaction, you will run around like a chicken with your head cut off. You will do and say things that are not true and are not productive. Further, you will be unable to listen to the other person or yourself. Being in reaction makes you a crazy headless chicken. No good can come from approaching a conversation when you are in that state. Being in reaction is akin to being temporarily insane. No court of law would label you insane, but effectively, you are acting like a crazy person. You are not yourself when you are in reaction.

You will have to notice when you are in reaction. It's important not to accuse yourself of any wrong-doing. Being in reaction is natural. It's not a sign of weakness or failure. It's a sign of caring and suffering. Once you recognize that you are in reaction, you can make the decision to break the spell and get out of reaction. This has to be a purposeful decision. In your mind, you will need to decide to stop everything you are currently doing to get out of reaction. It will take your entire focus.

Getting out of reaction is surprisingly easy when you are willing to do it. You have to be willing to notice all of the intense feelings in your body. When you scan your body, you'll probably find that your heart rate is elevated. Your stomach feels different than normal. Your skin might be hot or prickly. Maybe your face is contorted into a grimace or your fists clenched. All of these changes take place when you are in reaction. Feeling them and noticing them is the first step to breaking the spell. Don't judge any of these feelings. Notice them for what they are, simple bodily sensations.

Next, scan your psyche for emotions. What are you feeling? Anger, sadness, excitement, pleasure, superiority whatever it is, notice it. Again, don't judge any of these emotions. Anything you may feel is valid and true. By noticing and naming the emotions, you engage your ACC, which helps to calibrate the *Do something!* alarm that has been going off.

The *Do something!* alarm is like a fire alarm. When a fire alarm goes off, the fire department doesn't just start spraying water at the building. Instead, they check out the situation. They send a few first responders in to scan the floors of the building for fire. In doing so, they often find that the alarm was a false alarm and they simply get back into the truck and go back to the station. When you scan your body and psyche for sensations and emotions, you will find that you are not in grave danger. Emotions, no matter how intense, can't kill you. So you will always find that the first responders (of your emotional fire department) can get back in their fire truck and go back to the station.

Getting out of reaction can take somewhere between thirty seconds and twenty minutes. If you find yourself going into reaction when you are actively engaged in a conversation, you can let the other person talk while you scan your body. Alternatively, you can ask your conversation partner for a short break. You can go to the bathroom and scan your body there. Do whatever you need to do to get out of reaction. In reaction, you are not an effective communicator. You are likely to make the situation worse if you try to communicate while you are in reaction. So, taking the time to break the spell of reaction is well worth whatever time it takes.

Some situations are so troublesome that you find yourself in reaction even when you are alone, just thinking about the problem. Noticing your body and emotions will break the spell then too, but you can use the insanity of being in reaction to your advantage when you are alone. Being in reaction can be a great tool to tap into the beliefs that are hard to find when you are thinking rationally. When you are in reaction, you will mouth off about things that you didn't realize were connected to your current problem. You can find a great deal of insight while being in reaction when you are safely away from other people. Often your perspective shift will happen when your emotions are raw and heightened, as they are when you are in reaction.

When you find new perspectives, there's no need to seek evidence to prove that your perspective is right. The point of seeking new perspectives is about having flexibility of mind. For perspective shift to work, you can't be worried about being wrong or right. To practice the skill of perspective shift, you have to accept that there are many, perhaps infinite numbers, of ways to be right. Focus on flexibility when you are aiming for new perspectives.

Whose job is it to change the dynamics of the relationship? You might be in a conflict with another person and your first response to reading this chapter is to say, "Well they should be the one to change their perspective, not me." If this is your stance, then you do not currently have the appetite to deal with this conflict and that is ok. Take some time. Notice that you have the desire to resist changing. Be with that resistance. You don't have to rationalize it. If resistance is the truth of how you are feeling, then notice that resistance and do nothing.

Your appetite is your willingness to overcome challenges on your way to a goal. Whether it's pizza, a multimillion dollar payout, or a repaired relationship, it's important to work within the bounds of your appetite. Overreaching, and trying to do things you aren't willing to do, will doom the whole endeavor to failure. To stay in integrity, be honest with yourself about what it will take to move forward. Don't try to do more than you are willing to do. Shift your perspective until you identify the path between where you are today and where you want to be, then determine if you have the willingness and the appetite to get there. Only then, is it responsible to go forward.

## Summary of Key Concepts

- The belief of separateness creates suffering. Shift this belief to see that you are distanced from the things you desire so you can find a path to get there.

- Being distanced from something does not cause suffering. Instead it creates motivation.

- Your appetite is your willingness to do the work to complete the goal. Assessing your appetite is a continuous engagement. New information will come in and you'll need to decide if you still have the appetite to continue.

- To stay in integrity, don't set goals unless you are willing and able to accomplish them. Being out of integrity affects your whole life, not just the one thing you failed to finish.

- No project or problem is too big to accomplish when you have the appetite for it.

- Shifting your perspective is a fundamental step in accomplishing hard goals and changing damaged relationships.

- The secret to ending conflict between two people is understanding that both sides are silently agreeing to behave in a certain way. To change the dynamic, you can change your perspective. Remember that you can't pretend to change a perspective, you must actually see things differently to get a different result.

- To get out of being in reaction, use noticing to scan your body for sensations and emotions. When you do this, you send your emotional fire department back to the station for a few minutes.

# 4 - Fortress of Belief

*It's not denial. I'm just selective about the reality I accept.*

Bill Watterson, Creator of Calvin and Hobbes

Conjure, in your mind, a tower full of riches. The fortune might be material wealth, but it might be something else entirely. Whatever it is, it's exceptional and abundant. This fortune is locked away, high in the tower, surrounded by a labyrinth of walls, and protected by a series of moats filled with hungry crocodiles.

Your hero's journey is about to get hairy. The life you want is contained inside that tower. Your hopes, dreams, and future happiness are bound there and waiting for you to release them. You are ready. If you weren't, you wouldn't have read this far. Readiness is not the same as knowing how you'll proceed. Readiness is simply wanting what's in that tower. You don't know what harrowing trials you will face to achieve your goal. Each time you face a new barrier, you will have to ask yourself whether you are willing to go on. You can make that decision only when you have the knowledge of what's immediately ahead. Your sole burden is to accept responsibility for your choice to go forward or turn back. The choice is yours and yours alone.

If you're wondering who built this fortress and hid your hopes and dreams away, look no further. You built it yourself. Each wall was built as you went through your own trials and tribulations of life. Abuses, accidents, loss, miscommunications, hurt, emptiness, those things are the machinery that manufactured those walls. The walls are reinforced each time you defend your own behavior and blame your actions on the past or on others. The moats grow deeper every time you cite reasons for not following through with what you said you were going to do. The crocodiles grow hungrier and more vicious when you wear your adversity like a badge of honor.

These walls are a sham. You thought you were building them to protect yourself from danger and from others, but that's not what they do. These walls stop you from connecting with your own exceptional life locked away in the tower. They reinforce the illusion that you are separate from your desires. You built these walls to protect your dreams from the outside world, but look around. Standing outside your fortress, you are the only actor. There's no one else here. No one can hurt you or steal your fortune. The real question is whether you'll let yourself reach it. Or will you busy yourself with the maintenance of fortress walls forever?

Every barrier you see in your life is a wall in your fortress. One of those walls was built to represent how little time you have. Another was built to remind you that you don't have enough money to follow your dreams. Still another was built when you found yourself disappointed by a date who didn't show up and you decided that you never wanted to feel that way again. Another was built when you didn't get the job you wanted.

The walls look sturdy. They are thick, heavy, stone walls, but each have a vulnerability. If you can find it, you can bring the wall tumbling down. The rubble will remain as a memory of your constrained past, but the barrier will be gone forever. If you can remove all of the walls, you have free access to the tower and everything inside. These walls have a structural flaw. The weakness is that each wall rests on a keystone and if you find a way to dislodge that keystone the wall can no longer stand. In junior high, when you realized that people weren't laughing at you like you thought they were, you dislodged a keystone and a wall fell. When you discovered that your parents make mistakes just like everyone else, you dislodged another keystone. You've already crumbled many walls. You know how to do this.

Keystones are beliefs that you hold dear. You can call them key beliefs. When they are wrapped up in a wall of reasons and logic, they seem so accurate, valuable, and important. When you identify them and look at them out of context, they can seem silly. You learned these key beliefs early in life as you learned how the world works. You might have added a key belief or two as you grew up and learned about the adult world and romantic endeavors. If you experienced a trauma like war or violence, you might have added another key belief about that experience. Key beliefs can't be turned on and off as situations change. You live by them just as you live by the rules of gravity. Your key beliefs define the laws of your world.

Here are a few key beliefs held by various people who explored their beliefs during the writing of this book:

- I must hide who I really am, to protect those I love.
- I am responsible for the happiness of those I love.
- If I do well in school, I'm abandoning my ancestors who were oppressed.
- I was raped so I'm not responsible for my emotions or behavior.
- I don't need to smile; joy is private anyway.
- I can't enjoy myself because someone might die.

Separated from their supporting reasons, these beliefs are obviously not on par with a law of nature like gravity. They are not the truisms that their owners think they are. When a belief is nestled deep in a wall supported by reasons and defenses, it seems like an important rule to live by. Abstracted, beliefs seem like the musings of a crazy person. You have your own set of beliefs that hold up the walls in your fortress. They are different than these, but likely sound just as odd when taken out of context.

We all build walls and maintain them in spite of our desire to reach the tower. We do it because the walls provide structure that helps us predict what will happen next. It feels uncomfortable to be unsure. Being right feels so good and not knowing what might happen feels so bad. Those walls may stop us from achieving our goals, but they also act as protection from the winds of uncertainty. If you live among the same barriers each day, you know what will and will not happen. Uncertainty is kept to a minimum.

To reach your tower, you will have to turn all (or most of) your walls into rubble. Your fortress will have no structure at all if you take down all the walls. Without the structure of fortress walls, you can't predict what the future holds. Without walls, your fortress is a pile of historic rubble and a tower of fortune. Your life will be different without fortress walls and you can't know in advance what it will be like. How badly do you want to find out what your life is like when you aren't limited by your own beliefs? Do you have the appetite to reach that tower of fortune?

The winds of uncertainty feel scary. The unfortunate truth is that no matter how high your fortress walls, accidents still happen. People get sick and die. Economic downturns occur. Jobs disappear. No amount of wall building will prevent those things from happening. No amount of safe living, stable decision making, and future planning will prevent accidents and chance from taking away some of the things you love.

You maintain these fortress walls because they feel like protection. They feel important. You built them initially to create safety. You are able to argue at great length about why your walls are legitimately important. Reasons are your defense weapon. When you defend a wall with reasons, it grows stronger. If you are pushed to defend your wall until you have no further argument, you will end with this final argument, "Because that's the way the world works." That's what you'll say. The tricky part is that the argument is reversed. Your world works that way, because you built that wall, not the other way around. The world works in different ways for different people, all because of the walls they build. The world is full of double standards because each person sets his or her own barriers.

The secret to destroying a wall forever is to figure out what it's doing for you. Once you understand, and can say out loud what that barrier is doing to benefit you, you can make the informed decision to let both the benefit and barrier go. The wall will crumble into rubble and you will be a lot closer to your fortune.

Take the first belief from the list above as an example. "I must hide who I really am to protect those I love." This belief came from a real person who is able to hide his non-traditional sexual orientation from a conservative family and community, but unfortunately, finds himself also hiding his true value as a potential employee from employers when he's job hunting. Hiding is hiding. When you are good at it, you won't be able to stop. Accepting that there's no need to hide, will allow the hiding to end in all situations. When he's willing to be his authentic self to his parents and the world, then everyone will be able to see his value. Until then, he hides both the good and the bad.

The fortress in your mind is a mirror of the way that you see the world. Whatever barrier is in your way in life, that barrier has a corresponding wall in the fortress of your mind. In your life, and in your mind, that barrier feels insurmountable. Each wall exists, because you put it there, you reinforced it, and you continue to maintain its existence. You put it there because it seemed like it was a protection, and it probably was at the time, but you now see it as a barrier and it's time to consider crumbling it. As fantastical as it might seem, the way to move forward is to first crumble the barrier in your mind and then watch the real-life barrier crumble in response. Attempting to take on the world while you still have a belief holding you back is a recipe for suffering.

Key beliefs can be based on any kind of idea. There's no limit to the false laws that your mind can create for you. Beliefs are so unique that I can't list all of the possibilities here. You will have to discover them for yourself. Instead, this chapter includes a list of the beliefs that bolster key beliefs. Key beliefs are personal and a little bit crazy sounding whereas bolstering beliefs are tame and common in comparison.

Nobody discusses key beliefs in polite company. However, bolstering beliefs are public and acceptable to discuss. People tend to find bolstering beliefs that they can discuss with friends and coworkers, but those beliefs are just polite code for the real barriers in their minds. Take as an example, the last key belief in the list above, "I can't enjoy myself or someone will die." Unfortunately, someone did die while this woman was enjoying herself and thus the belief was created. But she would never talk about her key belief. Until she discovered it, the belief was hidden, even from herself. Instead, she used a bolstering belief about dietary restrictions and how dangerous it is to eat refined sugar. Bolstering beliefs are the superficial challenges in life that everyone can understand. It's important to remember that bolstering beliefs aren't the real problem, they are the polite problems that you pretend to have. Diets are polite to discuss. Death is not. So, we turn to bolstering beliefs as cover for our real key beliefs.

It might seem far fetched at first, that someone would take a deeply serious belief about enjoyment triggering death and exchange it for a superficial belief about diet and sugar. There's no logic in the connection between the key belief and the bolstering belief that people use to cover it up. Key beliefs and bolstering beliefs are unrelated issues. The only connection between them is the set of feelings that a person has attached to them. In this case, the bolstering belief about diet and sugar feels like an issue of life and death to the specific person who created it. She connected her experience of death to a belief about sugar. We have the ability to attach any feelings to any beliefs. Fortunately, we can also make the decision to disentangle feelings and beliefs too.

Solving a bolstering belief problem doesn't end painful feelings in the long term. At best, putting effort toward a bolstering belief can bring temporary comfort. We do get temporary feelings of relief when we indulge in entertaining our bolstering beliefs, and relief is a significant form of enjoyment. However, relief is fleeting. The woman who was using a restricted diet as her bolstering belief, can have an ideal diet and she will continue to obsess about improving it. Any enjoyment she gets from turning down a candy bar is short lived.

Bolstering beliefs are often huge or unsolvable problems. The man who was hiding his true self from his friends and family used a bolstering belief too. He obsessed about financial injustice in the world. In public, he discussed poverty and his plans to solve financial injustice. Each time he thought about ways to end poverty in the world, he got a little bit of enjoyment simply from the act of thinking about that topic. Financial injustice and this man's desire to hide his sexuality are unrelated issues, but he had connected them in his mind. Every time he felt the pain of hiding his true self, he would seek out thoughts about financial injustice so he could find relief.

Your mind hides your key belief deep in the fortress wall and puts a set of surrogate beliefs out in front. We all do this. We complain publicly about looming and insurmountable issues in our lives when those things are not the real problem. The bolstering beliefs act as substitute problems and those get all our attention.

Bolstering beliefs are about publicly acceptable problems that everyone can understand. People will obsess about time, money, food and other limited resources. Publicly acceptable beliefs can also be about identity. You've likely heard someone say, "As an artist...." or "As a scientist...." Which loosely suggests that someone's identity changes the laws of nature for them and the community to which they belong. Another bolstering belief is about how things should be done. You might hear people obsessing over perfection or doing something the right way or the wrong way, as though there were laws of nature that govern everyday activities. Another bolstering belief that drives a lot of people's behavior is the belief in an authority that controls their choices. Instead of recognizing the innate authority that each person has over their own behaviors and actions, people often cite an outside authority as the reason for their behavior. Surely you've heard someone do this. "I'll be late for our dinner reservations. My boss won't let me leave work yet." Bolstering beliefs are so commonplace that you will certainly recognize them. If you don't yet, you'll soon begin to see them. You'll likely even catch yourself using them after reading this chapter.

Although key beliefs are the real barriers, they aren't easy to see. First, you have to become familiar with these decoy beliefs. Bolstering beliefs are not the real source of the conflict in your life, they only look like they are causing you trouble. As you search for your own key beliefs, you will have to learn to look past these publicly acceptable beliefs. If you get bogged down in limited resources, identity, the right way, or an external authority, you won't be able to continue on your hero's journey. This is your first trial. Notice your bolstering beliefs.

## Limited Resources

One morning I awoke to a LinkedIn post by actor Keanu Reeves. It was a photo of himself on a busy street with people walking in the distance behind him. In the caption he wrote about how the people behind him were rushing to work without paying attention. He went on about how it's important to take a time-out now and again to say *hi* to someone. He wrapped up the post with a few motivating lines about making everyday count. The post was friendly and average as far as motivational posts go. What struck me was not the motivational message, but the comments from readers that followed.

The post inspired some bitter comments that illustrate what's going on with people when they are in reaction. LinkedIn is a professional networking site, and the comments tend to be about work or career. The majority of the comments spoke to the fact that Reeves is a wealthy actor who doesn't need to work and he can take all the time-outs that he wants. These comments basically stated that having resources (money, or time) allows for time-outs and not having resources disallows for time-outs. One of these comments struck me as a particularly detailed argument for how a lack of time and money prevented the comment writer from taking a time-out.

The comment author, I'll call her The Commuter, wrote the following:

> "[You can take a time-out] unless you are in Vancouver and you have to get to work on time so you don't get fired! 'Cause the transit system has let you down again and you can't afford to live in the empty homes worth 3 million in the city.... I guess if I were rich I might have a lot of time on my hands to consider these deep thoughts and of course slow down because I wouldn't need to work every day for 9 or 12 hours on a working wage. Capitalism has a funny way of speeding people up literally."

The Commuter wrote voluntarily and without a specific prompt. She saw Reeves' post in her LinkedIn feed just like I did. Thousands of people saw the post, and only 50 people had commented at that time of the morning. She was one of them. Thousands of other people scrolled past the post without reading it, or read it and didn't have another thought. Something inspired her to take the time to write her comment. She was in reaction.

The Commuter shared her beliefs about how the world works. There's no point in me proving her beliefs right or wrong. Doing so wouldn't benefit anyone. Her comments do provide an opportunity to examine how people cover up their key beliefs with palatable complaints that sound reasonable and logical. Bolstering beliefs are the decoy complaints that people use so that they can share their problems without getting into the painful key beliefs. We generally accept these complaints at face value. If The Commuter were your friend, you might have a conversation with her about how your commute is terrible too. You'd both be talking about your problems on a superficial level. Why do people do this?

Key beliefs are connected to intense and often painful feelings. Bolstering beliefs are connected to feelings that muted and are therefore less intense than the feelings of key beliefs. We are wired to move away from pain unless we have some compelling reason to move toward it. Although we can't ignore our conflicts and key beliefs entirely, we can stifle them and focus on a less intense decoy instead. Bolstering beliefs aren't the real problem and the brain knows it. The emotions connected to a bolstering belief are subdued in comparison to the intensity of the emotions associated with a key belief. When we think we can't deal with the pain of a key belief, we turn to bolstering beliefs instead.

---

### Exercise: Compelled to Comment

If you comment online, or in conversations in person, about anything at all, you can learn a lot about yourself by noticing what triggers you to comment (or like, or +1).

To begin: The next time you find yourself making a comment, notice the situation. What triggered your comment? What was your comment about? How did you feel before and after making the comment.

Why this works: Noticing your own behavior is a valuable part of becoming more aware. You are motivated by some things and not by others. Commenting is a voluntary endeavor so asking yourself questions about your own motivations is enlightening.

Pitfalls: You might discover that you comment so readily that you can't see any patterns in your comments. Highly active commenting is a pattern in itself. Notice how you feel when you comment. Try not commenting. What does that feel like?

---

The emotions associated with bolstering beliefs are less intense than those associated with key beliefs, but they are painful nonetheless. Consider The Commuter who was experiencing a painful set of emotions. She was compelled to complain about her problems publicly on LinkedIn. Her actions suggests that she was in reaction. Her ACC was shouting, *Do something!*

*Do something!*, is a difficult command to uphold when you are sitting on a commuter train headed to work. What actions are available to you in that moment? You can get up and start screaming. You can cry. You can get off the train. You can decide you'll never take the train again. You can complain. And that's the action she chose to take. The Commuter felt a big wave of feelings and took action by complaining on a LinkedIn post.

Complaining in a public forum is an action that doesn't solve anything. She knew that. To take the sting out of what she was feeling, she translated her emotions into rational thoughts. She took all that energy from stress, frustration, anger, disappointment and fear, and she put it into her logical reasons for those emotions. A certain kind of relief occurs when you shift your focus from the discomfort of your emotions into the reasons for your emotions.

A thought can't hurt you. No matter how awful, thoughts are just words. The hurt comes from the feelings that are attached to those words. Feelings can hurt you. Feelings can be painful. Your heart can pound in your chest so hard that you think you might have a heart attack. You can get so hot and sweaty that you might vomit from the discomfort. Your head can pound. Your vision can narrow. Your chest can tighten. Feelings are scary and seem dangerous. Emotions feel like they can hijack your body and make you do socially unacceptable things like sweat, cry, vomit, and scream. In contrast, thoughts are toothless. They have no way to bite you. They just sit in your mind and cause distraction.

Translating all of your emotions into reasons makes them less scary and less likely to cause you to behave inappropriately. We do this every time we say, "I was angry *because*...." Those magic words translate the pain of the emotion into the logic of the rationalization. Once the pain is translated into words, it can be stored in your brain as a key belief or a bolstering belief. This is how we get many of our beliefs; an emotional experience was translated into some bit of rational thought and stored away as a belief. Each time we encounter a similar set of emotions and sensations, the associated beliefs come back up.

Any associations between beliefs and feelings (feelings is used here as a collective word meaning emotions and physical sensations) are unique to you. Beliefs and feelings aren't naturally connected. Any connection you have between them was created by you at some point during your life. The Commuter had an association between the specific set of feelings she felt that morning and beliefs about time and money.

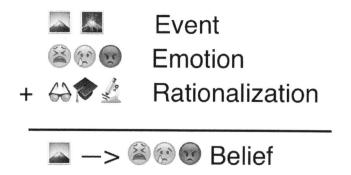

Event
Emotion
Rationalization

Belief

Fig 5. – Beliefs are born when an event inspires emotion and the event and emotions are brought together as a composite memory. Subsequently, the composite memory consisting of event and emotion are processed into an idea about how the world works; this is a belief. The belief is that all future similar events are sure to bring about the same set of feelings. Beliefs support future judgments like, "Events like this bring about bad feelings therefore these types of events are bad." To let go of a belief, you have to reverse the steps. You will have to be willing to notice and feel whatever emotions are attached to your ideas so you can separate the feelings away from the events. Feeling emotions, without rationalizing them, allows the feelings to disappear.

What does this all mean? Your beliefs are not what they seem to be. Beliefs act as a storage system for feelings. Translating your feelings into beliefs works for a while. You don't have to deal with your feelings right away and you start building up a library of beliefs. If you keep rationalizing your feelings and turning them into beliefs, over time, you will create a lot of beliefs. Inevitably some of them will conflict with your experience of the world. When this happens, the challenged belief becomes a conflict in your brain and you get a rush of feelings along with it. Unfortunately, this storage system isn't permanent. Feelings that were translated into beliefs aren't stored permanently, they are just dormant for a while. Each time that belief is challenged, the feelings come back.

The Commuter felt the discomfort of her stored feelings when she read Reeve's post. His world, where people have the freedom to stop and say *hi*, directly conflicted with her world where she was too grumpy and busy navigating public transportation to be friendly. Was she mad at Reeves?

No. Her feelings had nothing to do with him. He's a stranger to her. Was she mad about her job, or money, or time? Probably not. What was she upset about? There's no way for us to know without talking to her. It's possible she doesn't know when she created her beliefs and what caused her feelings in the first place. Were she interested in solving this conflict forever, she could use her bolstering beliefs about time and money as a starting point to unlock and explore her feelings.

Think about The Commuter's fortress of beliefs. A few of her beliefs are listed in her online comment; I bolded them in the text below so they are obvious. Each one acts as a barrier in her life. The more she defends them, the bigger the barriers grow. They feel insurmountable to her. The Commuter's barriers are not laws of nature that everyone has to deal with. These are her own personal barriers that she created each time she translated a set of feelings into a rationalization.

> "[You can take a time-out] unless you are in Vancouver and you **have to get to work on time so you don't get fired!** Cause the transit system has **let you down again** and **you can't afford to live** in the empty homes worth 3 million in the city.... I guess **if I were rich I might have a lot of time** on my hands to consider these deep thoughts and of course **slow down** because I wouldn't need to work every day for 9 or 12 hours on a working wage. Capitalism has a funny way of speeding people up literally."

What does The Commuter's world look like? She worries about being fired. More so, her ability to manage her time is crucial to her job stability. She feels let down. She can't afford to live and she imagines that if she had money, her life would be vastly different, slower, and somehow deeper. The truth is that money and time are not related. Buddhist monks have time, but no money. Corporate executives have money and very little time. Her beliefs are not laws of nature, but they are true to her and by holding on to them, she lives in a difficult world.

To avoid conflict, The Commuter probably spends her time with people who have similar beliefs and similar barriers. If she spent time with people who disagreed with her (like Reeves) she would be confronted with views that challenge her own. Experiencing conflicts associated with those beliefs would unleash feelings similar to the feelings she had at some point in the past when she created the beliefs. Since she doesn't yet want to deal with those feelings, she maintains and defends her beliefs.

When The Commuter is ready to remove the barriers in her life, she can do so. She can start by confronting her bolstering beliefs about time and money. Whatever feelings she has connected to those beliefs would come flooding back to her. Instead of ignoring those feelings, she could notice her sensations and emotions and experience them. She could use ACC exercises to calibrate her threshold for emotional pain. She could use noticing to stay out of reaction.

Limited resources are very common bolstering beliefs. It is socially acceptable to complain about the limitations of time and money. However, both time and money are fungible meaning that they can be shifted to accommodate changes. Said another way, schedules can be shifted, and appointments canceled to allow more time for a desired task. Budgets can be expanded or expenses tightened to allow for more money to spend on a desired item. When a person complains that they can't afford something, it often means they don't want to figure out how they might afford something. When someone says they are too busy, it means that they are unwilling or unable to figure out how they might shift their current schedule to accommodate the new event or task.

Taken to an extreme, you can look at time and money as the ultimate set of flexible resources. Someone like Tom Higley, who knows he is limited only by his appetite to connect the dots between himself and what he wants, knows that time and money aren't true limitations. If Tom needs more time, he finds a way to clear his schedule. If that doesn't fulfill his need for time, he starts looking for help from other people. He delegates tasks to family, friends, or volunteers. You can do this too. A task as simple as picking up your dry cleaning can be delegated to a friend who drives right past that dry cleaner each day. The 30 minutes you saved in delegating that task can be spent enjoying time with that friend over a glass of wine. Get creative. The limitations exist only in your mind. There is always a way to make more time.

When you hear yourself use the bolstering beliefs of limited time and money, notice the circumstances. See if you can leave these bolstering beliefs out of your everyday language. If you find yourself saying, "I can't afford to go to that restaurant." You can say, "I choose not to spend money at that restaurant." Instead of saying, "I can't go to that meeting."

You can say, "I will not make it to that meeting." Instead of saying, "I'm too busy too look at that report this week." You can say, "I will look at that report next week." Then be sure that you do what you said you were going to do. Leaving bolstering beliefs out of your everyday language will let the fortress walls retreat in your mind. When you don't reinforce them every day, they lose power over you.

# A Good Job

Conflict in the workplace can be minor or extreme. In benign cases, people quietly deal with frustrations and in extreme cases office conflict can escalate to violent levels. One pervasive conflict in the workplace occurs when everyone involved means well, and the more well-meaning they become, the larger the conflict gets.

People tend to set self-abiding rules and parameters about the jobs they do. As long as they work within those parameters, they give themselves a pat on the back. When they fall short, and break their own rules, they get upset and work harder to do what they have deemed is a *good job*. Working to a set of parameters or internal standards sounds like a great way to do good work, but problems occur regularly with this strategy.

Creating an internal standard for your own work can be an effective way to achieve great things, however internal standards can backfire. You can get so focused on achieving your own goals that your own goals become the only goals on your mind. Internal rules, parameters, and goals cause conflicts when they don't fit smoothly into the bigger picture. When you are compelled to do a good job, and forget to pay close attention to the bigger picture, you can cause conflict with well-meaning hard work.

Humans aren't the only ones who get caught up in their own internal idea of what it means to do a good job. Dogs have been bred by humans for thousands of years. We chose to raise and breed those individual dogs that worked well with us. Over countless generations, we developed a creature that is more human-like in their quirks and behaviors than like the animal most closely related to it, a wolf. Dogs are a reflection of human hang-ups. We can see our foibles in their goofy ways.

A dog named Roman started causing trouble in his neighborhood when he began attacking the neighbors. He viciously protected anyone in his family by barking and nipping anyone else who came near. The family had to call a dog trainer to work with him. After an assessment the dog trainer pointed out that Roman had given himself a job and that job was to protect his family. Roman's effort was tremendous and he had become a huge pain in the neck.

To solve the problem, the family had to give Roman a new job, one that everyone could live with. They bought him a doggy backpack and filled it with something heavy so he'd be sure to feel it. They put water bottles in the backpack and took Roman door to door so he could drop off one bottle at each house. He took to his new job with gusto. He stopped nipping and chasing people and he delivered water bottles like the neighborhood emissary. After a while Roman wore his backpack on walks and that was enough to remind him that he was a friend of the neighbors and not their tormenter.

Roman was dedicated to doing a good job, but when he wasn't given a job, he gave himself one. He created his own parameters and rules. Roman took it upon himself to decide that he had to bark at and nip at everyone outside the family. That self-directed job didn't fit into the community very well. It took a skilled dog trainer to see what was going on. Roman wasn't a bad dog. He was a good dog with a bad set of parameters for the job he gave himself.

People do the same thing. It's easy to get focused on working toward parameters of a job only to discover that those parameters have become a barrier to success. Take Alan for example. He was hired as a phone salesperson and his job was to get a decision maker to talk to him so he could pitch the software he was trying to sell. He'd call a company and get an operator. He would get transferred up the chain of management until he found his target. Alan had to talk to 4 or 5 people before he had any chance of getting in touch with the right person. Often without warning, the phone call was over before he connected with the person he wanted. He rarely got to talk to the decision maker.

Alan had given himself a job that was remarkably similar to the job he was hired to do but with a slight twist that prevented him from achieving the original goal. He was hired to sell software over the phone. The job he gave himself was to talk to the decision maker. It might seem like talking to the decision maker is a necessary step in selling software, and this was exactly Alan's argument for his actions. He became so focused on connecting with the decision maker that he forgot to connect to the other people he was talking to. He treated the people in between like they were barriers to his main goal.

Empathy works over the phone too. When the people on the other end of the line spoke to Alan, they received the unspoken message that he thought of them as barriers. It was a natural move for each of them to play the part of a barrier while they were on the phone with Alan. They weren't conscious of it, of course, but this is what happens when you treat someone as though they have a role to play. They generally comply. Each person he talked to acted like a barrier and rarely helped him get what he wanted. The people on the phone were eager to do a good job too. They did a good job of standing in his way. That's the job Alan gave them to do.

To improve his sales quota, Alan had to create a positive relationship with each person on the phone. No matter their corporate title, Alan had to see them all as a part of the solution. Alan started treating everyone as a decision-maker. He realized that each person had the power to make a decision. They would either hang up on him, or pass him to someone higher up in the company. Alan didn't have to come up with any cheesy lines to get people on the phone to understand. He genuinely wanted to talk to them and they could tell that his desire was real. Alan learned that it's nearly impossible to hide your agenda, even if you don't say it out loud, so it's important to make your agenda something that the other person will appreciate. Alan started having notably greater success in connecting with people who were in charge of buying software. He also started to realize that purchasing decisions are rarely made by one person alone. He saw how valuable it was to have a relationship with 4 or 5 people in his customer's company since those people tended to ask each other's opinions when it came to making big purchases.

When you think things aren't going well for you, stop and ask yourself what job are you doing. You might find that your attention has shifted to doing a job that is hindering your success instead of helping. Nearly everyone is doing a good job at something. You might be doing a good job procrastinating, sneaking smoke breaks, looking busy, or giving the appearance of being successful. When you aren't achieving your goals, check and see that the goals you think you are working toward are the same as the goals you are actually working toward. Most often the case is that you are highly successful at whatever job you gave yourself. That job might not allow you to reap the rewards you thought you were aiming for.

Conflicts occur when you work very hard at the job you gave yourself, but continually fail to reach your goal. You might be confused about what's going wrong. You find yourself saying, "I'm working so hard!" Maybe it seems like your boss, family, or the world is standing in your way. The trick is to recognize that your efforts have gotten you to where you are today. If you think your life has gotten off track, then you might have given yourself a job that is a bit askew of the job you need to be doing to reach your goal. Realign your job and your goal before doing any more work.

Look into your belief fortress. Is there a wall that is dedicated to doing a good job? Do you try to work hard to get ahead in life? Do you think that you will eventually have a comfortable life if you just work hard and put in effort? The belief that doing a good job results in having a good life is a bolstering belief that creates barriers for a lot of people. Like Alan, your efforts might be sabotaging your success.

---

**Exercise: Aligning Jobs with Goals**

You can fool yourself into thinking you are working hard toward your goals when you've actually gone askew of your original track.

To begin:
1.  Write down all your main goals that you put effort toward on a regular basis. When you are done, go back through the list and choose the one that you are putting the most effort toward right now.
2.  How do you put effort toward that goal? List the tasks that you do to accomplish your goal.
3.  Write down the barriers to achieving your goal. What stands in your way?
4.  Make an argument about how a specific task that you do can create the barriers that you listed.

Why this works: Life is complicated. It's easy to get blinded by the importance of tasks and forget about the big picture. Do regular checks to see if the tasks you are doing might actually be inhibiting your progress. Pay more attention to progress than to effort. Effort can be easily misdirected.

Pitfalls: If you can't see how you are standing in your own way, you are missing something. Everyone creates their own barriers. It's human nature. Becoming aware of the connection between your barriers and your actions is the first step to overcoming barriers.

---

# Knowing, Perfection, and the Right Way

Do you feel like you need to know the answers to questions? Do you focus on perfection? Is there a right way to do things? These are three seemingly benign beliefs that cause an incredible amount of pain for those who maintain them. Perfection is impossible, no one can know everything, and when you think there's a right way to do something, it's difficult to let others do things in their own ways. People who maintain these beliefs experience regular conflict and find that relationships are dominated by stress. These beliefs create standards for your life that are impossible to achieve.

There is no bigger barrier to discovering something new than thinking you already know it. I remember standing nervously outside the conference room where my PhD candidacy exam was being held. I had to convince five professors that I was capable of being a PhD student after spending a year in classes and another year planning the experiments that would ultimately make up my doctoral thesis. Two advanced students saw me in the hall and came over to give me moral support.

They looked at me and said, "You know how to pass the exam, right?" It was an oral exam. I had to present my proposal of experiments and defend how my work, when complete, would contribute to the field of neuroscience. I looked to them to confirm my hunch. They looked at each other and back at me. They said quickly, "Be sure to say, 'I don't know.' Otherwise you fail." I was floored. What? Really? I'm supposed to say that I don't know the answer to something and that's a requirement to pass?

It's true. A PhD student sets out to study something that no other person has studied before. The results of those experiments are unknown until the experiments are run and the data analyzed. If a student proposing those experiments is unwilling to accept that she doesn't know what will happen, then it is impossible for her to have an open mind. In an American school system that encourages students to know specific answers, the PhD candidacy exam is the first time a student is tested on their willingness to admit they cannot know the answer at this time.

Admitting that you don't know is hard. Think about it. It's not just a hit to the ego, although it is that too, it's admitting that you don't know what you are looking for. How can you find something when you don't know what it is? How can you do a good job when you don't know what you are doing? Not knowing is frightening on many levels, especially when you have grown up in an education system that rewards right answers and punishes you when you don't know.

Since the brain can only think one thing at a time, you can either know or not know. This means you can either be sure or be open to new information, but you can't be both sure and open at the same time. Said another way, you have a little switch inside that allows you to toggle your brain between thinking like a student and thinking like an expert. When you are the student, you are humble, quiet, and listening for new information. The student is not trying to prove anything. The student is like a sponge, soaking up advice and wisdom from the world. Flip the switch and you become the expert. The expert is sure, strong, and willing to share opinions. The expert shows how much she knows. The expert can fill the room with her thoughts.

Just like the brain switches between tasks, the brain switches between being the student and being the expert. Notice which state you are in. Pay attention and see. Are you the student or the expert right now? Is it easier to be one that the other? If you find yourself in expert mode often, you may benefit greatly from a purposeful switch to student. To be the student, find a humble feeling inside and listen without judgment. Judgment, after all, is the role of the expert. If you find yourself acting as a student most of the time, switch to expert on occasion. Share your opinion. Be strong in your knowledge.

Eventually, you will find the right times to be the expert and the right times to be the student. You will learn to speak and be bold in your knowledge when you have something to say that is both true and helpful. Other times, you will learn to be humble and quiet so that you can listen to the wisdom of the world around you. Remember, the expert cannot learn. Fortunately, you can switch between these two states of mind many times in a single conversation. Those who can flip the switch between student and expert can be adaptable anywhere.

The ability to flip the switch to become the student is one way to overcome the desire for perfection. To believe in an ideal of perfection, you must believe that you are the expert and that you can identify what perfection is. The moment you think you know what perfection is, your mind closes to anything else. You are then limited to being able to appreciate only that version of the world that your brain manufactured. Everything else becomes unsatisfactory.

You have a better chance at finding something amazing if you haven't predetermined how it will be when you find it. Keeping an open mind is remarkably hard. An open mind has no preconceptions and no judgments. It might help to remind yourself that any knowledge of perfection that you may have is an illusion. The moment that you settle into your comfort of perfection, you are settling into a fool's paradise that leads to conflict more often than not. Your version of perfection will inevitably conflict with your experience of what is. The desire of perfection is a recipe for suffering.

When you loosen the belief of perfection up a bit, you have a belief that there are right ways to do things. Perfection is an extreme, and many see its pitfalls before they fall in. Believing in a right way, however, is common. Few people are willing to forge their own paths for fear that they will step off the *right way*. Those who are able to retire their belief of the right way can break off of the beaten path to find opportunities that aren't available to those who still hold that right way belief.

Kiara Imani Williams is a professional woman in her mid twenties who made the decision to step off a traditional legal career path so that she could design her own way through life. She took a year-long break during her time at University of Virginia School of Law to get non-legal experience in the entertainment industry. After earning her JD, Kiara began working as a Legal Fellow at Public Broadcasting Service (PBS) in Alexandria, Virginia, which is a job that doesn't pay nearly as well as other job offers that she rejected after graduation. Kiara could have taken a job as an attorney in a firm, but she chose PBS. She has $200,000 in student loan debt and she took a non-profit salary that won't pay off those loans for a long time. Kiara knew her choices limited her salary only in the short term. After about a year at PBS, Kiara moved to Los Angeles to join Creative Artists Agency where her dual focus on both law and entertainment will surely benefit her achievements.

Kiara writes for the Huffington Post on the side. You can read her articles about her life as a beauty queen, her identity as a young black woman, and her vision for affordable education. If you feel inspired to write her a comment, be aware that she doesn't read them. She says that many of the comments are mean spirited and she chooses to stay clear of that negativity. Kiara is on an unusual career path and her choices tend to create conflicts for those who have beliefs about how a career should go. Her readers are often in reaction when they comment and their notes are hints into their belief systems.

One common belief that pops up a lot in the comments at the end of Kiara's posts is the *sunk cost fallacy*. You may have never heard this phrase, but you probably know the belief. The sunk cost fallacy says when you've spent money on something, it's important to get good use out of it. If you buy movie tickets, it's important to go to the movie. If you bought a gym membership, it's important to use the gym.

The sunk cost fallacy is used in response to Kiara's posts by people who can't stand that she makes career decisions that don't always use the degree that she spent money on. Many people believe that the right way to make career decisions is to make choices based on what you've invested time or money in previously. Any diversion from an original career plan, like Kiara's desire to focus on entertainment sometimes instead of law, conflicts with some people's belief about having a career the *right way*.

An economist would argue in Kiara's favor of doing whatever she wants with her career no matter what she spent money on in the past. The economic view is that once money has been spent, the cost should not influence your future decisions. If Kiara were to tie herself to a traditional law career simply because she got a law degree, then her education would be an effective barrier in her life. Under those rules, her law degree would limit her to law-related jobs and disallow her to take other opportunities. Spending $200,000 in tuition to limit your career options seems like a terrible waste of money. Fortunately, Kiara knows her education wasn't wasted and she isn't controlled by any of these beliefs.

There is no right way to have a career. There is no perfect career and all possible paths can lead to the career of your dreams. Career superstitions abound and they create barriers for those who believe them. You can find superstitions listed on career forums online. Beware, subscribing to beliefs about career paths does nothing more than create barriers for your career development. People claim you have to stay in a job for two years before you can leave. If you take a job, you can't quit right away even if it's a terrible fit. You must stay in your career field. If you switch fields people won't take you seriously. If you don't have a big salary right out of school, then you will never make a lot of money. Full time employment is the right way to have a career. You have to work and save so you can retire comfortably. All of these are beliefs that create barriers for those who subscribe to them. The barriers don't exist for people who ignore these beliefs. It's amazing what people can do when they realize that none of these restrictions are laws of nature.

Kiara knows that the only thing she has to do to have a great career is to follow her appetite, just like Tom Higley who bounced from being a musician to a lawyer to an entrepreneur. She isn't caught in the barriers of belief like the people who comment on her blog posts. Instead, Kiara can work at PBS until she is ready to do something else. When she determines what her next thing will be, she will determine how distant she is from it. She will draw a line between where she is and where she wants to be, then she will decide if she has the appetite to walk that line. Kiara has purposefully designed her life with a fluid identity and a willingness to see money and other resources not as barriers, but as shiftable and changeable realities. She is not bound by some predetermined notion of the perfect career. Kiara knows she's more likely to do something amazing if she admits that she doesn't know what it will be.

# Authority

As children, we are raised knowing that our parents have authority over us. This is a legal authority that gives parents and guardians the right to make decisions for children. At 18 years old, that legal authority lifts and we are each responsible for ourselves. Some people retain the belief that another person is responsible for their decisions. Many pretend that their boss, business partner, spouse, children, or child care giver is the person who calls the shots in their life. Still others defer authority to non-sentient things like work, traffic, time, their health, weather, or technology. Notice the next time you give an excuse that your alarm clock didn't go off, the traffic was terrible, or you have too much work to do. Excuses allow you to develop and maintain the belief that you are not responsible for your own life. To keep up with your integrity, you will need to recognize how your decisions do indeed influence the outcomes in your life.

A very disturbing psychology experiment done at Harvard in the 1960s and repeated many times since showed that a person who believes he or she is acting under the authority of another person is capable of acting outside of their own ethical boundaries. Social psychologist, Stanley Milgram showed that 65% of people (men and women) were willing to inflict pain on another person as long as they felt that they were being obedient to an authority. His work was published in a paper entitled *Behavioral Study of Obedience*. This study shows that when you believe you are acting under the authority of someone else, your boss perhaps, that you are capable of behavior that you would never do if you recognized that you were responsible for your own actions.

Milgram's work was highly controversial. With the Holocaust still fresh in everyone's hearts, the notion that Americans could have acted with such evil as the German SS officers who followed Hitler's authority to kill millions of Jews was too difficult for many to accept. People started to realize that the Nazis didn't have to be evil people to do what they did. Perfectly normal, ethical people are capable of performing atrocities when they believe they are acting under the authority of another person. To do what they did, the Nazis needed only one person in authority willing to be unethical and the results trickled down through the ranks. The work suggested that the majority of the population contains the capacity to torture others if ordered to do so by an authority.

Milgram recruited two people as subjects to each experiment. One was the *teacher* and the other the *learner*. The person playing the teacher sat in a room with the people who were administering the experiment. The person playing the learner was an actor, someone hired by the scientists, who pretended to be a subject. He sat in a locked closet with a tape player. The teacher was instructed to teach the learner pairs of words like: blue dog, elephant skateboard, apple west.

The person playing the teacher was the real subject of the study. He or she believed that the study was testing whether punishment was helpful in learning. As is the case in most psychological experiments, the true subject is unaware that their own behavior is the focus of the study. The experimenters used this study to determine whether a person was able to inflict pain simply because they were acting under an authority. When the learner failed to pair the words correctly (this was planned), the teacher was instructed to shock the learner with increasingly painful shocks. The teacher believed that the learner had a heart condition and was in severe pain during the shocks. Remember, the learner was sitting in a locked in closet with a tape recorder.

The learner would play recorded exclamations of pain at preplanned times when the teacher flipped the switch to "shock" the learner. Each teacher heard the same sequence of recorded "Ow!" "Please stop!" "Let me out of here!" and so forth from the actor who played the learner. The teachers were allowed to stop at any time, but were asked by the administrators to, "Please continue." The teachers generally would go on. If they remained hesitant, the other prods were used in sequence, "The experiment requires that you continue" and still if they didn't go on the administrator would say "It is absolutely essential that you continue." The teacher generally did continue with those prods. If they remained unmoved, a fourth prod was used, "You have no other choice, you must go on." That prod generally ended the experiment. When people were reminded of the word *choice* they snapped out of the authority spell and were able to think for themselves again.

Milgram and the other experimenters were in disbelief of the results. Could it be that people are capable of doing horrifying things to another person just because someone said, "It is absolutely essential that you continue?" How could that be? We have free will and morals. We have our own standards of right and wrong. And yet, as they expanded the experiment to include more people, a third of the subjects were capable of giving shocks of intensities equivalent of human torture when they thought someone else was telling them to do it. All of the subjects were willing to give serious shocks of 300 volts.

This experiment suggests that we are all capable of inflicting pain on others when we believe that we are acting under the power of an authority. What, then constitutes authority? In the experiment, the subjects were paid for arriving in the lab, and told that they were free to leave at any time without having to forfeit their payment. In a sense, your boss has more recourse over your actions than the research administrators had over their subjects. If the subjects were willing to torture a stranger because someone in leadership said, "please continue" then what are you willing to do when your boss, a person who can actually fire you, gives you a directive? It's unlikely that you will be asked to torture someone with a shock, but you might be asked to work long hours, to make decisions that affect your family life, or to damage relationships that you would otherwise not wish to damage.

The subjects in the Milgram Experiment believed that they were acting under the auspices of someone else's authority and that simple belief allowed them to behave in a way that they personally didn't think was right. This is a disturbing quirk of human nature. To avoid doing something that you might find regrettable, be sure to take responsibility for your own actions, no matter who is claiming to have responsibility over you. By recognizing your own unassailable ability to choose your own actions, you will make decisions that fit within your own code of morals and ethics.

---

### Exercise: Deference to Authority

People regularly use deference to authority as a way to explain their own behavior. You probably do it too.

To begin: Consciously listen to yourself and others throughout your day. Look for examples of people pointing to an authority (other than their own authority) as a reason for their behavior. Look for statements like:

- Sorry, I'm late. Traffic was terrible.
- I have to leave. My childcare closes at 6.
- I don't like my job. My boss is a bad manager.
- I didn't finish the report. The client kept me busy with other work.

Why this works: When you use language that make it sound like you don't have choices in how you behave, you start to feel like you don't have choices. By shifting your language to embrace your own authority, you will see how much power you do have over your own behavior.

Rephrase the excuses above into language that embraces self-authority:

- Sorry, I'm late. I didn't give myself enough travel time to account for traffic.
- I have to leave at 5:30.
- I don't like my job, but I'm not bothered enough to improve my relationship with my boss.
- I didn't finish the report. I chose to let the client tell me how to spend my time.

Pitfalls: Deference to authority is so pervasive in our culture that you might have trouble hearing it at first. You may defend your use of this kind of language at first. If you do, notice your desire to argue that you aren't responsible for your own choices.

---

# Identity

The English alphabet includes vowels, a, e, i, o, u and sometimes y. Sometimes y is a vowel, but sometimes it acts as a consonant. Like the y, the belief of identity is a double agent. Identity is sometimes a bolstering belief, and sometimes a key belief. People do talk about their own identities in polite conversations and those superficial definitions of self can cover up deeper key beliefs that cause troublesome conflicts. However, it's common for most people to have a very deep set of key beliefs that are based in identity too. When you track down your key beliefs, you may find that you start and end your hero's journey with trials about identity.

This is how the hero's journey started for Melissa, a 20 year old college student at Case Western Reserve University. The journey began when she decided to change her college major. With a couple of semesters behind her, Melissa was academically flapping in the breeze. The only class she'd really liked was an Introduction to Programming, which meant that

Melissa liked coding software. The problem was that she didn't feel like she fit in with the people in the computer science department. If she declared computer science as her major, her classmates would be young men who had been programming since they were 10 years old. She didn't identify with them. Her first programming experience was decidedly post-pubescent. She wondered if they'd accept her and if she could be happy, and most of all, she wondered if she could catch up. Melissa experienced an identity crisis after she followed her interests and changed her major to computer science.

Ideally, Melissa would be able to feel equally comfortable in computer science or any other major. A shift from one major to another would feel like a natural transition and she could focus on her studies instead of her identity. There's so much to learn when you switch majors, or career, or fields. Why do we get caught up in identity instead of diving right into the work at hand?

Shifts in life are connected to shifts in belief cultures. The people in the chemistry department have different belief sets than those in the computer science department. When you attempt to join a community that has beliefs that are vastly different than your own, conflicts are likely to occur. If you maintain a belief that isn't shared with the community, you'll feel a conflict. Some communities hold beliefs that you don't want to share. If you try to join those communities, your presence will create conflicts for others.

By now, you probably recognize that conflict is unavoidable. It's everywhere and it's not fundamentally dangerous. Conflict does feel bad, but when managed properly, it can be a wonderful force of positive change. Moving to a new community, like Melissa did, is a great way to create conflicts that allow you to find your key beliefs. Remember, next time you are the new kid on the block, that you can use that conflict as an opportunity to learn a lot about your own beliefs.

Melissa found that the pressure to fit in was strong. She struggled to feel like she belonged. She felt like a woman without a country and a visitor on trial. Melissa wanted to be accepted by her new community, but she didn't know what being accepted was supposed to look like.

Mentorship and role models are a great solution to the problem of fitting in. When a mentor can guide you in relationship building and help you see new ways of thinking about things, fitting in seems so much easier. A fellow student at Case Western, Hannah acted as Melissa's mentor and role model. She encouraged Melissa to go to the Grace Hopper Conference that was held in Phoenix, AZ that year. This conference is specifically for young women who code and has helped many young women through their own identity transitions to becoming the proverbial *Woman in Technology*. Hannah knew what it was like to add computer science to her own identity. Through mentorship, she helped Melissa do the same. Hannah now lives in Seattle and works for Google.

In Melissa's original mental image of a computer science major, she pictured a young man who talked a lot about coding languages, hacked his computer in high school, and cared more about software than dating. Hannah helped Melissa update her beliefs about computer science majors to include a young woman who worked tirelessly on software projects she loved, meeting people across the world through coding events, all while looking good in a dress.

Melissa's identity challenges weren't all about fitting in. Some of her problems included concerns about her own performance, which is common for anyone entering a new community. Being new to a field guarantees that you won't perform like an expert. Newbees have to go through growing pains, no matter how smart and capable they are. You have to expect a drop in your ability to perform when you join a new field where you are a novice. As you already learned, people fundamentally want to do a good job. The pressure to perform well causes many people to pretend that they know what's going on when they don't. Pretending creates conflict.

A big challenge for Melissa was to overcome her desire to be at the top of her class in a new major right away. Melissa had created beliefs about what it meant to do well in school. She found that she was less able to immediately excel in computer science classes, other kinds of classes were much easier for her. She was afraid that she'd set herself up for failure in school by switching to computer science.

About a year after the shift, Melissa had fully embraced her computer science major; she spent her free time writing blog posts about computer science and organizing coding events called hackathons. She hung out in the student lounge that is designated for electrical engineering and computer science students. She had subscribed to the social protocols associated with the community.[13] Although she's walking the walk and talking the talk, she still feels like an imposter. She feels like the real deal only when she's outside her new community talking to non-majors or new coders. When she's with what she calls "hardcore CS hackers" she feels like she has nothing to contribute.

Melissa shared some insight into her remaining challenges. She said, "I still feel like I have nothing to contribute beyond my people skills and ability to get things done. I'm still working on establishing my technical skills and experience so I can feel like I can also bring new knowledge to [the computer science community]."

Melissa is unwilling to call herself a real computer scientist until she can contribute new knowledge to the community. That's a tall order. New knowledge generally comes from expert level participants. Those just learning the ropes have a lot of rote knowledge to pick up before they can spend time innovating. Melissa created a barrier for herself. She can't fit in until she's an expert. That's going to lead to many years of discomfort. When Melissa decides to let that belief go, she will feel instant relief and acceptance.

Imposter syndrome is paralyzing and distracting. People with imposter syndrome feel like they don't belong, they don't have the qualifications to do what they are doing, and they are worried that they will soon be discovered. At the heart of these concerns are key beliefs about what it means to belong.

Melissa benefited from her belief that she wasn't yet a real computer science student. To allow herself to be computer scientist right away, she would have to accept that she was one of the most unskilled and inexperienced members of her community. While she maintains her status as imposter, she doesn't have to face her neophyte foibles. However, pretending is a recipe for suffering. It's hard to accept that you stink at your new field, but it's worse to spend time with people and

---

[13] An example: when asking for help from other computer science students you have to prove that you gave the problem a good effort first.

pretend you aren't really part of the community. That kind of pretending damages relationships.

---

### Exercise: Identity

Your identity is a strong driver of your behavior. When you can step back and notice your identity, you can see how you might behave differently if you weren't trying to fit into a role.

To begin: Make a list of all of your identities. Try to get to 20 or more. Here's the start of the list I made for myself: *Artist, Writer, Woman, Free spirit, Scientist, Thinker, Independent, Athlete, Competitor, Guru/Mentor, Student, Expert ...*

Then go through the list and say to yourself: "I am not an Artist." "I am not a Writer." "I am not a Woman." With each statement, see how you don't fit the characteristics of what you are supposed to be like according to that identity.

Why it works: Stepping back from your identity allows you see how you have, not one, but many identities and that they are each important and also unnecessary. You don't have to maintain an identity to be who you are.

Pitfalls: You might find that you are simply going through the motions with this exercise instead of deeply exploring how you don't fit the identities you picked. Notice your reaction to this exercise. Is it boring, pointless, or interesting? Notice your emotional response to being asked to do this exercise. Are you resistant? Accepting?

---

Everyone has a wonderfully unique personality and personal history that makes them special. We enjoy people based on these unique differences, but we get can get carried away thinking that personality is the most important element dictating our behavior. In fact, behavior is different from personality. Personality is indeed unique. Behavior is learned.

Identity is neither personality nor behavior. Identity is an idea, a set of thoughts, that define who you think you are. Identity can be about religion, education, race, nationality, gender, age, generation, music, sports, fashion, or anything else that people rally around. Your identity includes the concept of yourself and the concept of groups you belong to. Identity also includes your beliefs about the way the world works for your community of people.

Identity is not a law of nature. It's a comforting set of beliefs that allows you to feel connected to your family or community. Your identity is always an illusion. Like any other belief, your identity feels as real as gravity and that's the problem. People tend to argue that their behavior is unchangeable and fundamental to who they are as a person, but it's not true. All of your behavior is changeable, no matter how deeply rooted it feels. You can find the belief at the bottom of the undesirable behavior and decide whether you will keep the belief, or if you would rather retire the belief along with the behaviors it causes.

You learned your identity as you grew up. Some elements of your identity were bestowed upon you by family and your community. Other parts of your identity you designed on your own. The truth is that you can't be defined by your identity. At your core, you are something more fundamental than your identity could ever define. There is a spark of life inside you that has no history, no name, no gender, no career, and no future plans. Your spark of life is the difference between a lifeless body and you as a living breathing person. Your fundamental self doesn't need a title or resume. That self doesn't have traits or desires. You are a valid, accepted, connected human simply because you are. Identity isn't necessary.

Don't worry. You don't need to let go of who you are. Instead, you can recognize that you are so much more than your identity defines you to be. Find ways to make your identity more flexible. Recognize that you have many different facets of yourself and they are all changeable. When a facet seems like it's more of a barrier than a positive force, consider whether you can let that one go.

The bolstering beliefs described in this chapter are just a few of the publicly acceptable surface issues that people use as surrogates for what's really going on for them. As you investigate your own beliefs, you can begin to discover the layers of beliefs that make up your fortress walls. The closer you get to the key belief, the more emotion you will feel. You might find anger, sorrow, irritation, incredulousness, betrayal, compassion, elation, or anything else. At first, the beliefs you find will all be bolstering beliefs. It's fine to understand them and let them go. This understanding allows for chinks to form in the fortress wall, which weakens the wall and gets you closer to the key belief. Don't stop learning about your beliefs until you have found the key belief. Pretending you found the key belief when all you've found is a bolstering belief is a surefire way to end your progress. Pretending the wall is gone when it's still standing tall is an unhelpful delusion. Keep looking to see what's inside you. This is not a race.

# Summary of Key Concepts

- Your belief fortress is unique. Each wall was built as you went through the challenges in your life.

- The world works in different ways for different people, all because of the walls (or beliefs) they build. The world is full of double standards because each person sets his or her own barriers (or beliefs).

- The secret to destroying a wall forever is to figure out what it's doing for you. Once you understand, and can say out loud, how that barrier benefits you, you can make the informed decision to let both the benefit and barrier go.

- Limited Resources are one of the publicly acceptable conversation topics that people use as decoys to protect themselves from their real beliefs.

- Good Job beliefs convince you that you are doing a good job, even if your efforts are not moving you closer to your goals.

- Knowing, Perfection, and the Right Way are a set of beliefs that guide people to seek a ideal. These beliefs distract you from great opportunities.

- A belief that you are not your own Authority creates the chance for you to make decisions that are harmful to yourself or others because you don't believe yourself to be responsible for your actions.

- Identity is a set of beliefs that seem like they connect you to other people. It's hard to let go of identity beliefs because of the illusion that you lose touch with your community or yourself when you do.

# 5: Uncertainty

*The bad news is you're falling through the air, nothing to hang onto, no parachute. The good news is there's no ground.*

Chogyam Trungpa Rinpoche

Although your barriers are unique to you, one barrier is shared by everyone: the discomfort of uncertainty. It stops people in their tracks time and time again. Uncertainty feels terrible to everyone. Uncertainty is the experience of not knowing, not feeling like you have enough information to make a decision, and not having a solid idea of what's going to happen next. The experience of uncertainty activates the ACC. You get the message, *Do something!* You feel like you don't have enough information to make an informed decision but your brain wants you to *Do something!* That contradiction is enough to create a conflict.

To purposefully grow, change, or to point your life in a new direction, you must be able to experience uncertainty and not go into reaction. When you are in reaction, you are no longer able to listen to the options that are available to you. To purposefully direct your own life, you can't get spun around every time you don't know all the answers.

Uncertainty feels bad, but it's not actually dangerous. Ideally, you'd be able to feel the spookiness of uncertainty and instead of feeling like you needed to *Do something!* about it, you'd just notice it. You'd recognize the subtle differences between feeling uncertainty and feeling danger. Further, you'd be able to use the feelings of uncertainty to navigate through uncharted waters. Each time you feel uncertain, it's a sign that you are embarking on something truly novel to you. When you get used to feeling uncertainty, and become comfortable with the discomfort of it, then you can use those feelings to your advantage.

You'll have to overcome some hurdles to get comfortable with the discomfort of uncertainty.

A safe and secure life is an illusion. Accidents and misfortune happen randomly and there's nothing you can do to minimize the chances below a certain baseline of avoiding risky behavior. Life is both risky and uncertain and much of your life is controlled by chance. Notice that I wrote that life is *both* risky and uncertain.

Uncertainty and risk are not the same. Risk is a measurable probability that something will or will not happen. Risk is definable. There's a risk that your company will downsize next quarter if profits don't increase. There are two potential outcomes. In one outcome, the company keeps the corporate structure that they have. In the other outcome, the company lets a lot of employees go. Management probably knows exactly what sales have to occur this quarter to keep the employees on staff. Uncertainty is unknowable. You don't have enough information to guess what might happen. If you leave a career without lining up a new job, you can't know what job you'll get in the future. You don't have enough information to know all of your potential job options. You certainly don't have enough data to know your probability of landing a specific job. There are too many unknowns.

## The Devil You Know

Daniel Ellsberg is an economist.[14] He found that people irrationally avoid uncertainty. Given two otherwise equal choices, one that is clearly defined and the other containing unknowns, people will overwhelmingly choose the clearly defined option. Unfortunately, we also tend to choose the clearly defined option when it's less valuable than an unknown. How

---

[14] Those well-versed in history and politics will remember Daniel Ellsberg for his famous Pentagon Papers in 1971, but his early career contributions to economics and the psychology of decision theory are of interest in this chapter.

much are we giving up in life, when we blindly avoid options containing unknowns?

We don't need fancy economics experiments done at Harvard to know that people avoid the unknown. Many cultures have a way to say this. *Better the devil you know than the devil you don't know.* In Peru, the saying goes, *Más vale malo conocido que nuevo por conocer.* Basically, human nature tells us to go with the things we know, even if we don't like the things we know. Ellsberg tested human decision-making by putting people in situations where they played games of chance. He observed the choices that his subjects made. Based on careful game design and observation, he uncovered what we now know as the Ellsberg Paradox which is, that people will choose a less valuable option when the more valuable option contains unknowns.

Although Ellsberg's experiments took place at the economics department of Harvard, I propose we examine his findings with a more stimulating backdrop: a Renaissance festival. Probabilities and wagers are more interesting when a busty wench is running the show! Imagine, the sun is setting. The smell of sausage and turkey is in the air. Tankards of ale are raised aloft. Let's place some bets!

The busty wench in question is Blue Bess Morgan and she's waving you into her tent. It's dark in the tent and it smells musty like the inside of an old trunk mixed with cloves and the greasy odor of sheep's wool. She has huge glass jars filled with ping pong-sized balls, but some are different colors, not just white. She holds up a scarf. "Take it." She says. You'll put the scarf over your eyes before you play the game. The first game is always the same with Blue Bess. If you reach into a jar and get a blue ball, you get $100. If you get a white ball, you get nothing. Bess is fair. She doesn't pull any tricks on her patrons. She's happy to let you trick yourself. Bess knows that people make self-defeating choices all the time. The first game is easy but you have to play all of Bess' games before you get your money. They get harder as they go. Ready?

With a flourish, Bess pulls a cord from the ceiling. A once grand, now moth-eaten, sheet whips around to reveal two jars. One of them is covered with an opaque silk veil and the other is clear glass. The clear jar is full of blue and white balls in seemingly similar numbers. Bess confirms what you suspected, with her slippery voice and waving arms, that the jar has 50 white balls and 50 blue balls. As if by magic, she makes a motion and the balls begin to stir themselves inside the jar. To the right of the clear jar is another jar of the same size that has been cloaked in a dark silk veil. The cloaked jar is also full of blue and white balls totaling 100. Bess won't tell you how many of each but she reaches in and pulls out two - one blue and one white - so you know that there are balls of both colors. Bess doesn't cheat!

To play, you pick a single ball from one of the jars. If you pick a blue ball, you get $100 added to your scorecard. Your goal here is to win money. If it isn't, then Bess chose the wrong patron for this experiment. Economics experiments make the assumption that you will make decisions that you believe give you the best chance at walking out with a bulging wallet. In all of these games, there is information that you know and there is information that is hidden from you. Some things are left up to chance, but not everything. You get to make choices that can improve or lower your chance of winning a cash prize.

Oh, one more thing. There are economists hiding in the shadows taking notes. They don't care how much money you win. They do care how you choose. The economists rock forward to see what you do next. Your move will be telling. Based on what you do know about the chance of winning between the two jars, there's no difference. Both have a 50/50 chance of giving you a blue ball. In the first jar, you saw 50 blue balls and 50 white balls - a chance of 50/50. In the second jar, you saw one blue ball and one white ball - a chance of 50/50. Of course there's a big difference in the level of unknown in each jar. Your ACC appraises just how much is unknown. The clear jar is devoid of unknown. The veiled jar is almost entirely unknown. Your ACC takes note of the difference. The economists lick their pencils with anticipation. Bess' first game is a simple one. You must choose one ball from one jar.

When Ellsberg was a student, he ran experiments just like the game in Bess' tent. Functionally, he was one of those economists in the shadows. When the majority of Ellsberg's patrons chose the clear jar, which is statistically no more likely to produce a winning ball, he started asking questions. Scientific breakthroughs happen when people question the obvious. Sure, people avoid uncertainty. We know this because we all do it. But why? What's going on? What drives these decisions?

Ellsberg created experiments that included obfuscations of information like Bess' cloaked jar did. He tested people's process of decision-making, not by asking them hypothetically what they like, but by giving them the chance to win a real cash prize. When people made choices that lowered their chances of winning money, he asked them if they wanted to try again. Sometimes they did, sometimes they didn't. He tried to get to the bottom of what they were thinking. The most powerful word in a scientist's (and economist's) vocabulary isn't *Eureka*, it's *Huh?* When an experiment doesn't give the expected result, there's something really cool to discover. But let's return to Bess. She's got another game ready for us to play.

As your eyes adjust to the dim light, you see a single cloaked jar. There is only one jar in this game. Bess tells you that there are 60 balls in it. She picks up the jar, shakes it, and gives you a look. Some of them could be black and some could be yellow, but she won't tell you how many of each are in the mix. She picks up a bag and, from it, she pours 30 red balls into the balls that were already in the jar. In this game, you bet on a color. In the first round, you can bet on red or black. Then Bess will pull a ball. If it matches your color of choice, you win $100.

Feel free to reason with yourself now. What is the chance of Bess pulling a red ball? You have 30 chances to get a red ball. What is the chance of her pulling a black ball? Eh, somewhere between 0 and 60. Black could be better odds or lower odds than red. Take your time. Bess can wait.

Which do you choose red or black? Remember your answer.

The jar with its obfuscated contents remain untouched for the next round. This time you get to choose two colors. Red/yellow or black/yellow. Take your time, you win $100 when Bess pulls a ball and it matches one of the colors you chose.

You know that there's 30 red balls and some unknown number of yellow. So, betting on red/yellow gets you a chance of 30 plus more.

You also know that there are 60 balls that are either yellow or black so betting on black/yellow gets you a known chance of 60.

Which do you choose?

Most people choose red in the first round and black/yellow in the second. Ellsberg noted this overwhelming set of preferences. He also noted the fallacy in betting like this. Those who chose red in the first round and black/yellow in the second round are effectively making a bet *for* and *against* red. There is no change to the number of red balls, so why is there a change in desirability of choosing red?

It doesn't make a lot of sense to bet *for* and *against* the same thing. That's like going to Las Vegas, walking up to a roulette table and putting $100 on red, then before the Croupier has a chance to spin the wheel, you put another $100 on black too. You are bound to both win and lose!

It might be unclear why this this bet is for and against red because you are examining this game with a human brain that is susceptible to *uncertainty aversion.*

Notice that the two rounds of bets are exactly the same except for the inclusion of yellow in the second round. The first round, the bet was between red and black. The second round, the bet was between red/yellow and black/yellow. Since nothing changed in the jar between the first and second round, if you liked red alone, it would stand to reason that you'd like it with yellow too. Same could be said of black. If you liked it in the first round alone, you'd like it in the second round with yellow.

Ellsberg wrote about this work in his 1961 paper, published in The Quarterly Journal of Economics, called *Risk, Ambiguity, and the Savage Axioms.* Savage is the name of another economist; it's not a paper about wild beasts. In it, he describes a funny exchange with his fellow economists when he subjected them to Bess' game. Some economists bet *for* and *against* red too. Ellsberg was interested to understand why a smart person, educated in economics, might bet for and against himself. He made sure each person was clear about the mistake and then he let the economist reconsider his bet. He offered do-overs and asked subjects to explain their choices. He wanted to know what was going on. Why were people choosing irrationally?

Ellsberg's colleagues were people who recited economic theory like school children recite the Pledge of Allegiance. These are people who spent their days thinking about rules like *The Sure Thing Principle* and *The Principle of Insufficient Reason.* These axioms are used by economists to define the risk in a decision. Some of the economists followed the axioms from the start, reciting them as they chose, and made bets appropriate to economic theory. Others changed their minds to follow economic principles only when Ellsberg made them aware of their conflicted bets. Still a third group violated the economic principles "with gusto." Paul Samuelson, an economist known for quippy remarks, huffed that he would stick with his choice "to satisfy his preferences and let the axioms satisfy themselves." Why would someone make a choice that got him statistically farther away from having a chance to win $100?

Ellsberg, asks his reader, "What did *you* think you were doing? What were you trying to do?" What this experiment and other supporting experiments uncovered is that people tend to shy away from choices when there are unknowns. The red choice is known, so betting on it feels good. Black/yellow together outnumber red 2:1, but people feel uneasy about betting on black alone instead of red. Black contains a lot of unknown, whereas red contains no unknown. Sure, there's a chance that there are 60 black balls, but there could just as easily be none. The uncertainty of the black choice is enough to turn most people off. When you give the black/yellow option, people get excited about betting on black. The uncertainty is gone. The question marks are lifted. By adding yellow to the black bet to make the black/yellow bet, you ensure that it's a bet 2:1 over red. No brainer!

Ellsberg's experiments are simplified versions of life choices. It feels good to choose something that is known. It feels bad to choose something that is unknown. That feeling occurs because uncertain decisions activate your ACC. Uncertain decisions make your brain shout, *Do something!* You might interpret that message to be, "*Do something* to minimize risk of loss!" But that's not what your brain meant by *Do something!* Your brain meant, "The *Do something!* threshold was just triggered!" It's just a feeling. You don't have to act on it. It's a warning light. Heed it enough to understand where the feeling came from. Notice the feeling. Let the feeling diminish and then make your decision. You might find that your chance for making money goes up.

---

### Exercise: Uncertainty

Every looming future decision contains knowns and unknowns. The unknowns get our attention, but the knowns are more important to decision-making.

To begin: Identify a decision you will need to make without knowing all the details first. This might be about picking a school for your child, or about changing careers, or even about whether you want to get married.

Step 1: Describe the decision you need to make. Let's use a career change as an example.

> Decision to make: "I'm not sure I want to work as an academic scientist anymore."

List your choices:
1. *Stay in academic science*
2. *Move to industry side of science*
3. *Move to another career outside of science*

Give each option an uncertainty rating between 0 and 3. 0 is no uncertainty meaning that you have a lot of information about that option. 3 is a high level of uncertainty meaning that you don't know much about that option.
1. *Stay in academic science (0)*
2. *Move to industry side of science (2)*
3. *Move to another career outside of science (3)*

Why this works: Uncertainty feels uncomfortable and we tend to ignore choices that have high uncertainty ratings even when they are very valuable choices. When you explicitly denote an option as having a high uncertainty rating, you can see why you might not be taking it seriously.

Pitfalls: When an option has a high uncertainty rating, don't just write it off as a bad option. Do your homework to learn more about it. As you learn more, the uncertainty rating lowers and you might find that you are more excited about an option that seemed frightening initially.

---

# Making Decisions in Uncertainty

Claudia Batten was a 27-year-old lawyer living close to her parents in New Zealand when she decided she needed a change. She had a vision of what she wanted her life to be like. It was full of lipstick and stilettos, fashion and fancy parties and she knew where she needed to be, New York City. She got on a plane and moved there, but when she got to New

York, it was not what she expected. She now admits that she was deeply influenced by the television show, "Sex in the City." When she got to her new home, she realized that the version of New York that she'd created in her mind did not line up with the real New York. Not only that, but she didn't have a job and she didn't know anyone.

Claudia didn't go to New York in search of a good time. While she was working as an attorney in New Zealand, she had a few clients that were building online companies that sold products. She fell in love with online companies and wanted to do more with them. Instead of acting as an attorney for one of these companies, she wanted to be part of one. She wanted to start her own company. What might she sell? Claudia loved makeup so it made sense to her to start an online cosmetics company.

New York seemed like a great place to do such a thing. However, the harsh reality was that she had no contacts and no support in her new city. Claudia discovered that to go after her dreams, she was going to have to make her own way. Now you can easily find and read books about entrepreneurship by people who have started companies. They explain how they went about it. At the time that Claudia was living it, people didn't talk about these things. No one had coined the term *lean startup* as a method to innovate and launch a new company. Claudia had no instruction manual and no rules. She was in search of an exceptional life; she didn't want to track along some predetermined path. But how could she proceed with so many unknowns?

She discovered that uncertainty was a navigation tool that she could use to have a less ordinary life. She knew that she could feel uncertainty, somewhere hard to define, in her body. It was uncomfortable, but not life threatening or unbearable. She also knew that she only felt it when she was embarking on something novel to her. The feeling of uncertainty became Claudia's compass.

Many years later, Claudia now teaches others how to step into deliberate discomfort. She has found her own way to ensure that she has an exceptional life and she wants others to be able to do the same. She doesn't teach people to follow in her footsteps, instead she teaches about how to overcome the human foibles that hold people back. Claudia got comfortable with discomfort. She learned how to use it to her advantage. In her first few months in New York, her ACC told her to *Do something!* and she learned to use that alarm to serve her well. Instead of heeding the warning and seeking safe harbor when she felt uncertainty, Claudia started to seek out the spooky feeling.

Claudia learned that there are no big decisions to make. It's the little decisions that impact the trajectory of your life. It might seem like moving to New York from New Zealand was a big decision, but it wasn't. It was common for new attorneys in New Zealand to work for about two years and then move overseas to join a law firm somewhere else for a while. Claudia had to make the little decision of whether she was going to be one of the few people who bucked the trend of leaving the country. She liked the idea of living in a new place so that decision was easy; she would leave home. She chose New York; she had an affinity for it because of television. That was easy too. She chose not to get a job as an attorney when she moved because she wanted to work in a cosmetics company that sold online. That was just as easy as the other decisions. There were no big decisions to make.

Next, Claudia learned to take steps without first having a defined plan. She realized that she could be productive without knowing exactly what she was doing or where she was going. She knew she wanted to start a company. So, what did she do everyday to get her closer to her goal? How did she know what to do next? Claudia simply started doing things, anything at first. Every time she did something, she was able to see the next thing that needed to be done. It's like walking in thick fog. You can't see where you are going, but every step gets you a closer to something (anything) and when you are about to hit it, you see it. You can't know what's going to happen. You can't see into the future. It's possible to make uninformed decisions. We are hesitant to commit when there's uncertainty because the ACC is giving us a danger sign, but there's nothing dangerous about moving forward.

Uncertainties include unknowns, but they also include knowns. Think about Bess' games. There's a choice that is completely defined. The other choice is a mix of defined and undefined. This is the same in life. Uncertainties contain knowns too. Once you come to accept the discomfort of considering a choice with unknowns, you can look deeper into it. You can learn more about the knowns and you can make decisions based on those. Claudia learned to notice how unknowns made her feel, and when she felt the spookiness of unknown, she used that feeling as marker to remind her to seek more information. She made decisions based on the knowns that were mixed up with the unknowns.

Claudia didn't start a cosmetics company. Instead, she joined some people she met in New York who were starting some kind of company, but they didn't know what it was going to be at first. They moved through a thick fog together. The team made little decisions as they grew their company. They decided that they would stay flexible about what the company did until they had supportive feedback from customers. They decided that they would keep going, shifting, and flexing. They wouldn't take it as a failure if they didn't get customers with their first, second, or third ideas. They followed the customers and the money. There's no way they could have predicted what they'd end up doing.

In a few short years, Claudia and her team developed a company called Massive, Inc., that specialized in putting advertisements in video games. Advertisements were common in television at the time, but not in video games or even online. Massive, Inc. was the only company to do it initially. They were successful at attracting customers and within a short time, they sold Massive Inc. to Microsoft for a sum reportedly between $100 and $300 million. Claudia moved from being an attorney in New Zealand to a successfully exited startup founder in New York. She did it without making any big decisions.

What might have been different for Claudia if she didn't decide to get used to the discomfort of uncertainty? What if she felt that discomfort every day and ignored it instead of noticing it and using it as her north star? She might have gone forward trying to start a company with the people she met. She might have been successful, but she might have suffered daily, trying to fight herself into a place of comfort. The company might have settled on *Doing something!* that wasn't attractive to customers just so that she could feel an end to her discomfort. If Claudia bailed out of her discomfort by lowering the number of unknowns in her life, she would have felt better, safer, and more in control, but she would have had to sacrifice her desire to have an exceptional life. The life of exception is, by definition, different than one you can predict. The exceptional life is guaranteed to be full of unknowns.

After Massive Inc., Claudia built another company called Victors & Spoils. She again used her discomfort feelings as a guide when building that company. No, Victors & Spoils isn't a cosmetics company either.

Instead, she'd learned a lot about advertising through her time with Massive Inc. She used that experience to build a new kind of creative company. Instead of hiring creatives as employees, Victors & Spoils uses creative work from people all over the world to serve huge clients like Coca Cola, Harley Davidson, and American Express. She sold Victors & Spoils after a few years and went on to do other things. Claudia says that when she doesn't feel the discomfort of uncertainty, she knows she's not growing anymore, she's not pushing herself into something novel. Claudia has used this method time and time again to ensure that she leads an exceptional life.

# Seeing the Postcard

Uncertainty is always part of your life. There's always something you don't know about your everyday decisions; the world is too complex to know everything about what's going on around you. What happens if you try to ignore uncertainty and push through with what you are doing anyway? Uncertainty feels terrible whether you notice it or not. Chris Neale, the founder and CEO of Fracture ID, an oil and gas technology company, felt the discomfort of uncertainty when he was raising money for his company, but he had not yet learned the value of using it to his advantage.

Chris had built his company up to seven employees. They had customers and they were on their way to providing a popular service in the energy field. Chris had talked with investors who seemed to like him and his company. Raising money was time consuming and stressful and he was ready to move forward building his company. He felt like he was spending all his time talking to people about money instead of doing business. He also wished for his team to get past the natural spooky feelings that come with not knowing whether they had enough money to go forward with their plans.

Chris found himself in a conflict because he was ignoring uncertainty. This was similar to what Claudia went through when she moved to New York from New Zealand. She didn't know what she was getting herself into, but she *thought* she knew. In her mind, Claudia had created a postcard of her life in New York, but when she got there, it became clear that she had made it up. Her beliefs about her new life didn't match her experience. Chris encountered something very similar when he tried to raise money for his company. After signing some preliminary, and non-binding, documents with one set of investors, Chris developed a postcard in his mind about how his company was going. He imagined the investors giving him money, the company growing happily over the next year or so, and then he saw himself selling his company to a bigger company, much like Claudia did with Massive Inc. This vision of the future was a postcard from his imagination.

Chris had a lot of evidence to reinforce his postcard. He knew the investors he'd been talking to. This same group of investors had invested in his previous company and they had been highly supportive of his new company from the early days when he was first submitting a patent and filing incorporation documents. They even vouched for his technology when he was seeking a government grant. So, Chris knew that this group of investors liked him and liked his company. He knew that they were willing to publicly endorse him. However, investors don't always have the freedom to invest in a company just because they like it. Investors are bound by agreements that can prevent them from investing in something they like. Chris looked at the evidence that these investors had been supportive and had invested in him in the past. He ignored the truth; it didn't matter how much the investors liked him, his investment still wasn't certain.

Chris had some preliminary documents signed with the investors, but there was no promise of commitment. He had not yet secured the investment. When time dragged on and the company still didn't have money from the investors, Chris started to get uncomfortable. He had the discomfort of uncertainty blended with the pain of conflict. His experience did not match up with his beliefs about how his company was supposed to look. The postcard in Chris' mind showed seven happy employees with full salaries and an increasing customer base. In reality the employees were taking home half-salaries and they were uncomfortable because the financial future of the company was still uncertain. This conflict activated his ACC.

When his ACC shouted, *Do something!* he responded by looking more intently at the postcard in his mind. On the surface, Chris looked like he was working hard to keep his company growing while the investment process played out. A deeper look revealed that Chris was in denial about the status of funding.

Ideally, Chris would have been aware that people naturally freak out a little when they feel uncertainty. Instead, he had a belief that he was supposed to feel good when things were going well. When the uncertainty discomfort arose, he went into reaction. He assumed that discomfort meant that bad things were happening with his company. He created a postcard in his mind, which was a vision of the way his company would look when it had successfully raised funding. Each time he felt uncertainty, he turned to that postcard for comfort. The postcard was an idealized vision of his company and it felt good when he thought about the ideal outcomes of his efforts. If Chris had been aware that he would feel oogy, spooky uncertainty feelings as a natural part of doing something novel, he might have been able to stay out of reaction.

Months went by and the investors didn't make a move toward giving the company money. A lot of paperwork happens before investment. It's like buying a house using a mortgage company. There are phone calls and pages upon pages of signatures. If those things aren't happening, you know the process has halted. He could have easily known that his investment process had halted, but Chris was in reaction. He was living in his postcard. To get out of denial, he had to realize that things weren't as they seemed. As the expiration date on his original investment document approached, he started to notice his conflict. He started to feel the things that he'd been ignoring. It didn't feel good.

He was angry, disappointed, hurt, worried, threatened, and embarrassed. He was in charge of getting his company funded and he realized that he was much farther away from achieving that goal than he thought. He'd spent months staring at a postcard in his mind instead of working toward the goal. In the postcard version, his goal was already attained. It was hard for him to realize that it wasn't true. Putting down a postcard is like waking up from a dream. The manufactured version of the world dissolves and you can see what is.

Like any conflict, at first it looked like an unfair assault. He blamed the investors for leading him to believe that they were going to give him money. Of course it wasn't their fault. They didn't commit to giving him money and he knew that. It was important that he saw his own responsibility in the mistake. It would be hard for him to talk with new investors if he were feeling bitter about the last investor interaction. Any hard feelings that remained could potentially mar relationships with new investors. To see his own responsibility in the mistake he had to become flexible in his perspective.

It was only a matter of days before he gained clarity. Soul searching helped him see the belief that was triggering his conflict. He believed that growing his company was supposed to feel good. The company's success, development, and promising future logically added up in Chris' mind to a bunch of positive feelings. When he felt spooky feelings, he denied them and looked more intently at the postcard in his mind so it could inspire the feelings he thought he should be having. Once he realized that his discomfort feelings were normal, healthy, and an expected part of doing something new, he was able to reconcile his conflict and move forward.

He bought a plane ticket to visit some new investors. The last obstacle in overcoming the realization that you've been living in a postcard is to start living in the world again. This step is where integrity is fundamental. When you realize you've been staring at a postcard of your life, it can be jarring to snap into reality. You can't stop at feeling uneasy. You have to pick up and march on with life. Chris might have wallowed in self-blame, or created bolstering beliefs to save face, but neither of those choices would have gotten him closer to funding. Chris was able to learn about uncertainty, recognize that it was powerful enough to push him into reaction, and he was able to gracefully recover before any harm was done to his company or business relationships.

Six months after he discovered that he was living in a postcard, Chris' company closed $2M worth of funding with a different venture capital firm. The company was able to continue operating and growing during that six month period of time. No one else knew about Chris' journey through his postcard world. That was his private experience. Fortunately, he was able to reflect and see what was going on with himself. He was able to feel the emotions well up when his experience of reality didn't mesh with his postcard beliefs. He was able to get back on course within days and it paid off.

## Exercise - Postcard

A postcard is an idealized version of your world. Record your response to this exercise for audio or video journaling.

To begin: Choose some part of your life to focus on. Example - family, social life, career, or appearance.

Describe the idealized version of one part of your life. Talk about how perfect all of the details are. Don't lie, just highlight how great things are. When you are done, describe the same part of your life in a pessimistic, negative light. Again, don't lie, just focus on the negatives and all the things that could be improved.

Why this works: The reality of your life falls somewhere in between. When you are looking for positives, you'll find them. When you look for negatives, you'll find those too.

# Denial of Uncertainty

You may have noticed that denial has played a role in the stories here. Beliefs themselves are a form of denial; you convince yourself that you understand what is true. Mental postcards are an elaborate form of denial. Conflict, too, is a form of denial. To maintain beliefs, postcards, and conflict, you must be willing to deny.

Denial might feel like a harsh word. You might think about times when you've seen a friend in denial and they aren't in a good place. *Denial* isn't a judgement of character or health. Denial is something that everyone does sometimes. Recognizing denial and noticing when you are in denial is a big step toward getting free of it.

From Ellsberg's work, we know that people tend to choose the well-defined option even when the poorly defined option has a better known chance of providing value. The natural reaction to uncertainty is to deny it. We deny that the uncertain choice is a valuable choice. We deny that the uncertain choice is even a valid option. We deny, like Chris did, that feeling discomfort is ok. We deny that, in life, every choice contains unknowns. We pretend that some choices are less risky than others, when most of we call *risk* is actually uncertainty.

Denial allows things to stay as they are in your mind. Denial is superb stabilizing force, possibly the best stabilizing force that there is. When we have conflicts with others we deny the other person the validity of their perspective. Holding onto a belief is a denial that another person's view might be just as real as your own. The moment you can see a new perspective, your postcard version of the world fades ever so slightly. Letting go of denial is often accompanied by strong emotions. It is a natural part of the hero's journey to deny the journey at first. Overcoming your natural resistance is necessary to embark on the trials of the journey.

As you start to identify conflicts in your life and you begin to work through the concepts in this book, you might struggle to find your key beliefs. When you get frustrated because you haven't had a breakthrough, check to see what part of you is in denial. It can be tricky to shift your focus enough so that you can see that you've been looking at a postcard and not at real life.

Ideally, you can decide that denial isn't valuable to you. You can accept that uncertainty is spooky and uncomfortable and that you are willing to feel it while you grow. Your key beliefs will come to you over the next few months and you will address each one with grace, dignity, and integrity. Then you will live out the rest of your days awake and able to deftly navigate conflict. You will see the world as it is and accept all perspectives equally. Wouldn't that be nice?

There are some serious challenges ahead. You are embarking on something that is hard. Finding your beliefs is hard. This is not hard work, that's different. This is like willing yourself to wake up from a dream. This is like shifting your perspective in an optical illusion. This is like admitting to the world that you failed in a fundamental way. This is like looking for something when you don't know what it looks like. Those things aren't hard work, but they are very hard.

Those who embrace uncertainty are aware that the unknown is ever present. Uncertainty is a real part of everything. Many of the stories you've read in this book so far are from people who have embraced uncertainty. Chris Neale learned to navigate uncertainty while he was immersed in a half year long funding process. Claudia Batten learned to use uncertainty as her north star when she found herself alone in a foreign land. Tom Higley embraced uncertainty when he decided to use his appetite as a driver for his success instead of relying on an analysis of risks and chances. Kiara Imani Williams stepped into the unknown when she saw the possibility for her own exceptional life. Melissa didn't know what might change in her life when she became a woman in technology, but she pushed on in spite of that uncertainty. Notice as the stories continue how uncertainty influences decisions and directions. Notice how it affects your own life.

# Summary of Key Concepts

- To purposefully grow, change, or to point your life in a direction that is different than the one you are currently on, you must be able to acknowledge uncertainty.

- People will generally choose a less valuable option when the more valuable option contains unknowns.

- Uncertain decisions make your brain shout, *Do something!* It's just a feeling. There's no real danger.

- There are no big decisions to make. It's the little decisions that impact the trajectory of your life.

- When you realize you've been staring at a postcard of your life, it can be jarring to snap into reality again. You can't stop there. You have to pick up and march on with life.

- Denial is a superb stabilizing force, growth can't happen when you are in denial.

# 6: MindSET Presence

*I didn't arrive at my understanding of the fundamental laws of the universe through my rational mind.*

Albert Einstein

Ötzi is the name given to a 5,000 year old European mummy found in the Alps in 1991. Thawing ice revealed the body of this ancient man to hikers when they were walking beyond the dedicated trail. The mummy was so well preserved, that we have been able to learn a lot about ancient people from studying him. He wore clothes that were sophisticated in their construction. He even had on snow boots with insulation, and a design element for increased traction on slippery surfaces. He had arrows and a copper axe. Scientists were able to figure out what he ate in his last meals by looking at the contents of his belly.

This mummy provides a lifetime of research opportunities for archeologists and scientists to understand what happened in the past. We can identify true facts about Ötzi's life. Analysis of pollen in his gut, chemicals in his hair, and materials in his clothes give us undeniable evidence about the way he lived. His shoes, for instance, were so detailed in their construction that some scientists are convinced that Ötzi got them from a professional cobbler instead of making them himself. The truth is that we know his shoes were made with a highly detailed construction, but we don't know the whole story. We can't know who made those shoes. We never will, no matter how much we analyze the data. The full truth of stories is lost to time. Evidence from the past tells us only so much. What were Ötzi's intentions on the day he died? What were his hopes for the future? We'll never know.

The problem with the past is that we can't know everything about it. We can establish facts, but can never know the whole story. This partial narrative holds true even when remembering our own past. Much of what we call *experience* is lost to time. Feelings that happened in the past are translated into the memories of having had feelings. Recollection of an emotion is not the same as having that emotion now. Memories, even memories of emotions, are actually thoughts, not emotions. Emotion is in the present and memories are from the past. Your imagination is the only place where they can be together.

When you recall a memory, you conjure thoughts into the present. Memories have a life of their own in the present. They grow and change just like any other thing that exists in the present. Memories are not true representations of the past, they are changeable, interpretable stories that were inspired from the past. Memories can be implanted and modified without the knowledge of the person recalling the memory.[15] Memories have even be implanted biochemically in a laboratory setting.[16] Scientists have begun to pin down the molecular mechanisms that allow for memories to be recalled. Their findings suggest that each time you recall a memory, it changes. Memories are surprisingly malleable.

The past is gone, but constantly changing memories are with you always. Your current state of mind influences your memories and your memories influence your state of mind. Your brain creates a feedback loop of present and past. Here's an example of how this works. You may live next to you neighbor for years having a few interactions over that period of time. Then, you learn that he has been accused of some horrific wrongdoing involving children. You will be able to go back into your memory and pick out times when you saw your neighbor in close proximity to children. You might even be able to recall some sinister

---

[15] Elizabeth F. Loftus' life's work uncovered the disturbing fact that you can implant a memory into another person quite easily. Her famous "lost in the mall" study involved implanting a memory of being lost in a mall as a child. 37% of subjects were able to recall, in detail, events that had never happened.

[16] For a TED talk by the scientists who implanted memories in mice, search this - Steve Ramirez and Xu Liu: A mouse. A laser beam. A manipulated memory.

behavior on his part. The present news will not only heighten any accurate memories you may have about him, but it can also cause you to invent memories that never really happened.

Many people suffer with pain from memories that they would like to forget. Memories of lost relationships, traumas, and mistakes can create suffering in the present. When you maintain the belief that a memory is a true representation of the past, it's easy to blame that memory for your current state of mind. How you feel now, when recalling the memory, is often used as evidence to justify the wickedness of that memory. That reasoning simply doesn't hold up when you look at how memories work. Each time you recalled that memory, you changed it. A benign memory can get connected to anxiety feelings or deep sadness. This happens when you recall a memory while you are feeling these emotions, and subsequently draw a connection between the memory and your state of mind. After that, future recalls of the memory might include emotional pain when originally there was no pain in that memory.

Ideally, you can learn to use the malleability of memories to strip them of their power over you. Memories are not evidence. They are barely a shadow of the events that happened in the past. Some memories are completely false. Yet, as fallible as memories are, they can create barriers for you in life. Your memories exaggerate dangers, inspire fears, and create hesitancies. To break free of painful memories, stop believing them. They are not the truth.

Your relationships are influenced by your memories of others. Consider the loss of a loved one. That person lives in your heart through feelings and memories. Losing someone is painful when you believe that you are now separated from them. Remember, just like with maintaining positive benefits from your long lost teddy bear, you can maintain a benefit permanence with someone who has died. Even though that person is physically gone, their benefit to you lives on as long as you let it. Accurate memories aren't necessary to continue to feel the benefit of a person in your life long after you last saw them.

You hold memories of people who have died, just as you hold memories of people you saw last week. You hold inside you, a small version of each person who is important to you, and your memories and beliefs about them helped you to make that avatar that represents them. Just like memories, the imagined versions of your loved ones are not true. They change with your influence. If someone is causing you pain without even being in the room or otherwise present, check to see how the avatar of them inside you is perpetuating the situation. The real person is oftentimes not the cause of your pain. Your beliefs about them, and the avatar you perpetuate is the cause of your pain.

The past is gone, and in the present, we maintain beliefs about the past that affect us daily. To be able to be present, truly listen, grow, and have relationships with the real versions of our loved ones we must recognize how we each perpetuate the past. Memories of the past are not true. Memories of people are not true. Your memory of yourself is not true. Perpetuating the past, based on your memory is the same as living in an illusion.

Truth exists only in the present. The past is made up of opinion, extrapolation, and illusion. The future is made up of expectation and speculation. Facts may transcend time, but like with Ötzi's shoes, the facts don't tell the whole story. Reducing an experience to facts is like reducing the Grand Canyon to a postcard. A breathtaking wonder of the world compared to a small flat paper and ink object; there is no contest. It's time to learn how your life can be in the present. The present is magnificent.

## Jamming the Present

Present experiences are rich with information. In the present, you think and feel. Information comes to you in your eyes, ears, nose, and skin from everything around you. Emotions come to you from other people through your sense of empathy. Your mind processes and compares, it looks for patterns, and evaluates. Twinges, heat, pains, pressures rise up from your skin and muscles and guts. The body is a receiver of information that can be gathered only in the present.

Radio receivers pick up the information traveling on radio waves and turn that information into sound. A radio can pick up only the waves that are currently available. A radio doesn't have the capacity to go back in time to receive radio waves transmitted yesterday or last week. Your body is like a radio receiver. It picks up information in the present and turns that information into thoughts and feelings.

Radio receivers can be jammed with competing radio waves that produce noise or other nonsense information. When a radio is jammed, it doesn't transmit intelligible sound from the radio waves. It transmits useless noise instead. The human body's ability to receive and transmit the truth of the present can be jammed too. The truth is blocked when you adhere to beliefs. The truth of the present comes to you from the outside world and from your own body. Everything around you, and also your state of mind and body are all the truth of the present. Beliefs are not the truth of the present, but they can come to you at the same time as other information in the present. Beliefs are the jamming signal that prevent you from making sense of the present. Conflict is the noise that results.

Without the noise of conflict, you can hear the truth of each conversation. You can feel the connections of your relationships. You can see your opportunities and risks clearly. Your mind is quiet. The chatter of to-do lists are gone. Nagging internal voices go silent. Your urges and cravings dissolve. Questions are answered without words. You can just be. Mentally sharp. Productive or unproductive as you choose in each moment.

You can learn how to use your body as a receiver to be present. Many of us think of the body as a dutiful servant that follows directions (or ignores requests) to move certain ways, behave certain ways, and execute certain commands. Executing orders is only a small piece of what the human body can do. An important part your body's capability is receiving information. You may have yet to experience just how clearly your body can listen to the world without confusion. You, dear reader, are only a couple of dissolved beliefs away from being immersed in presence instead of being busied by noise and conflict.

Many people seek awareness and presence without recognizing that it's there all the time. Radio waves are ever present and the radio receiver is simply a way to collect and experience them. You are collecting information from the present all the time. If everything you experience doesn't feel clear and true, then your receiver is jammed. To get a sharper signal, you have to find the beliefs that are blocking you from experiencing the present in its full glory.

If a belief were truly like a keystone in a wall, you could find it, identify it, and destroy it. But a belief is an intangible and slippery thing. A belief is basically just a thought. The more you ache to throw away a thought, the more it tends to materialize uninvited. Where do beliefs come from? They don't start as thoughts.

Beliefs are born in an undertaking that looks a bit like hastily tidying up for unexpected guests. When you have only a few minutes to make your home presentable, clothes, books, and dishes are stashed with reckless abandon and no concern for order. Imagine a dirty dish that is shoved into an unused cabinet. You might forget about it, until it starts to smell bad and you can no longer ignore it.

At some point in your life, you had an experience that you hastily stashed away. A painful moment inspired strong feelings, maybe a long time ago. Instead of taking time for the experience and noticing the pain that it caused you, you ignored it. Your brain translated those feelings into thoughts and stored that experience as a belief. Over time, you started counting on that belief. Eventually, it grew in a status and became as important to you as a law of nature.

When you experience a conflict, one of these beliefs has been challenged. You might be willing to put up with little conflicts for a long time. However, when your belief and subsequent conflict starts affecting your family, marriage, job, or ability to find peace in the world, you will probably want to retire it. That belief is not serving you anymore.

To get rid of a belief, you reverse the process that was used to make it. Beliefs came from hastily tidied feelings, so to let go of beliefs, you have to feel the feelings that are connected to the belief. Don't worry, the past is gone. Whatever happened to create this belief is over. The feelings attached to it will be different, fresh, and not really the same as the ones you felt a long time ago. It might be a difficult experience, but just like dealing with that increasingly bad smell of the dirty dish in the cabinet, it's only going to get worse until you handle it.

# Three Channels of MindSET

A radio receiver turns radio waves in the air into music and news that you can tune into through different radio stations or channels. Your body (which includes your brain) does something similar through a three-channel system that I call MindSET. MindSET is an acronym of sorts that describes all three channels of experience: Sensation, Emotion, and Thought. These three channels of information work together to provide rich, present information about your world. If you are using all three channels together, you are sure to be present.

## Sensation

You can get vast information about the outside world through five of your senses: sight, hearing, taste, smell, and touch. You also get information about the position of your body through proprioception. Other sensations from your body give you status updates about your health, hunger, or hormone levels. You have sensory information about space, objects, and people. You can identify food through smell and taste. You can see beauty and movement and all kinds of complex things. You can feel hungry. You can feel your libido. The malaise of illness, the exalt of winning, and the cold sweat of fear are all sensations that give you information about the truth of the present.

None of these experiences can be directly translated into thoughts. If you had to describe the sensations associated with running very fast for three blocks to a logic-based robot, you'd find much of the verve lacking from your description. The robot might get a list of body parts and corresponding descriptions of sensations, but it's not the same as feeling it. The only way to know what it's like to have your heart pound, your legs get weak, and your lungs burn, is to experience it for yourself. Fortunately for me, you have experienced these things and so I need only remind you of that experience.

Sensation can drive behavior. A surprise tickle on your hand might make you jump. A grumbling belly can make you reach for a box of crackers. Libido makes you behave in certain ways that might raise (or lower) your chances of attracting a partner. You can feel how your body moves and responds during the behavior that you performed. You feel the food settling in your belly and the changes in your blood sugar. It's a complicated system of feedback loops. Close your eyes and move your arms. You still know where they are in space. Make a face. You can feel yourself quite clearly.

Bodily sensations can drive how you feel overall. Scientists have measured significant changes in hormone levels that were caused by physical sensations. Physical touch, especially skin to skin contact is known to increase the hormone oxytocin. This hormone is thought to create a feeling of well-being and bonding between individuals.[17] However, physical touch doesn't have to be related to affection; professional massage can increase levels of oxytocin as well.

Amy Cuddy, a social psychologist at Harvard, studies the effect of body position on overall feeling. She looks at the chemical reactions associated with feeling states that happen in the body. Her lab discovered that if you hold a specific body position for only two minutes it changes your hormones significantly. Cuddy's lab looked at both testosterone and cortisol levels in people who were randomly assigned to assume a high power position or a low power position. High power positions include positions where you take up space, hold your arms and legs out wide, or lean back in your chair with your arms folded behind your head. Low power positions include stooped, slumped, or crouched positions. Both men and women participated in her experiments, and hormone levels were checked before and after subjects spent two minutes holding the position.

High power positions triggered a substantial increase in testosterone and a notable decrease in cortisol. This means that after subjects held power positions, they felt more powerful and less stress reactive. Testosterone is a well-known power hormone. Less publicly known is that cortisol makes you highly reactive to stress. The subjects who adopted the low power positions (bent over, arms crossed, taking up little space) had the opposite change in hormone levels. Cortisol went up and testosterone went down. You can improve your overall feelings within two minutes by adopting a powerful position.

---

[17] For a TED talk about the implications of oxytocin in society search for - "Paul Zak: Trust, morality -- and oxytocin?"

Bodily sensations give you rich information about the world. You can learn a lot simply by tuning into the feelings in your body. Remember that sensation isn't a logical channel. You can't directly correlate a pain in your elbow to some meaning about the world. Instead, notice your sensations. Notice how you automatically behave when you feel different things. Watch your body like it is some exotic species that no one has ever studied. You might be amazed at what it's trying to tell you. The conversation can go both ways. If you don't like how you currently feel, you can use power positions or touch to feel better.

## Emotion

Emotion is a wildly sophisticated channel of information. Emotion is the first responding channel in any experience. You can feel emotions from other people, even strangers. You can have emotions long before you logically recognize that something is going on - we know this by looking at functional brain imaging. You can have two or more emotions at once. So the emotion channel of information is more elaborate than thinking since you can only think one thing at a time. Your emotional channel is so deeply in tune with the world, that it might seem that your emotions are out of step with you.

Culturally, we learn that emotion arises in response to events or memories and that the emotion is somehow owned by the person who feels it. Countless online articles are filled with advice about how to take responsibility for your own emotions. Unfortunately, this way of describing emotion limits learning and presence. You can't own or be responsible for emotions. It's not an accurate description of how emotions work. Emotions aren't your fault; they aren't the fault of others, and they are completely uncontrollable.

Taking responsibility for your emotions is often the sage advice given to someone who is upset that other people are making them feel certain ways. There is great comfort in believing that you can control how you feel and no one else has that power over you. Likely, though you have noticed that other people do affect you emotionally, no matter how much emotional owning you try to do.

**Exercise: Erasing Meaning**

We often assign meanings to our emotions. It's the meaning we assign the emotion that causes us trouble. Not the emotion itself.

To begin: Video journal or write a description of an event or conflict that is bothering you. Be brutally honest. This is for you. Be descriptive about what's not working for you and describe how you feel.

Then, go back through the video or journal entry and find where you've attributed meaning to your emotions. Look for statements like, "I feel angry because you didn't listen to me." or "Anyone else would feel the way I do." or "I'm sad because I didn't get the respect I deserve."

Why it works: Emotions are not logical; they are emotional. Giving a reason to an emotion turns it into a logical-type thing and stops it from being an emotion. Emotions process faster and dissipate quickly when they have no meaning.

Pitfalls: When you have an emotion, say, "I feel angry" or "I feel disappointed" and leave reasons for your emotion out of your expression. Even if you change your language to talk about emotions without using the word because, you might still be attribute meaning to your emotions. Notice how you think about emotions.

Emotion got a bad reputation at some point. People started equating emotional experiences with pain. That's not how emotions have to feel. Pain occurs when the ACC screams, *Do something!* When your ACC is calibrated and your beliefs aren't causing conflicts, emotions are not at all intense or painful. They are beautiful, colorful, and rich with information.

Emotions are the data on one channel of information that you can sense. You can use that information to learn about the status of yourself and your fellow human. Emotion has no owner and it has no definitive source. Emotion is influenced by so many things including other people, memories, beliefs, and culture that pointing to a single reason for an emotion misses the other (many) potential influences that are too complex to ever pin down. It's more accurate to say that we can't know definitively where an emotion comes from and therefore no one can own it.

Through empathy, you pick up the emotional states of others and you feel those emotions as though they were your own. There is no cognition needed for empathy. You don't need to put yourself in the other person's shoes in a thinking way. If you see someone crying from sadness, you feel sorrow. If you see someone having road rage, you feel anger. You don't have to think about it. It just happens. Thinking about the other person can ruin the effect. By thinking about someone who just lost a loved one, by wondering what it feels like to be in their shoes, you block your emotional experience and turn it into something thought-based. To know how someone feels, just look at them and then look inside yourself to see what you feel. You'll get a very clear picture of their emotional state by observing what, up until now, you believed to be your own emotional state.

Empathy is a new concept for many, but it is an ancient phenomenon. Empathy, the instant sharing of emotional states between people, allowed us to live as a social species that worked together for survival. What better way to respond instantly and as a group than to be able to share emotion without the use of language? In the face of danger, only one individual needed to recognize the danger and the whole pack of early humans responded with fear. In light of opportunity, only one individual needed to see the chance at catching food and the whole pack responded with the increased energy of excitement. To feel empathy yourself, begin to notice just how changeable your emotional states can be around other people. Simply walking into a room can influence the way you feel.

Since emotions come from others and also arise spontaneously in you, they are messy and complex. Emotions are a channel of information separate from logic (thinking), so there's no way to assign meaning to emotions. You can pick up an emotion from a passing cyclist. What's the meaning in that? The emotion channel works best when you recognize that emotions are never rational. They are never justifiable. Emotions don't have reasons for existing. They simply exist. When you justify a reason for your emotion, you end its life an emotion and turn it into some feelings-associated logical thing. A reasoned emotion is sent on its way to become a belief.

To keep emotional information in its own emotional realm, refrain from assigning reasons for emotions. Instead of saying, "I am angry because you drank all of the milk." You can separate the thought from the emotion. "You drank all of the milk. I feel angry." It might seem like semantics, but your brain knows the difference. In the first case, your anger is assigned to the milk incident. In the second case, there was a milk incident and there was an emotion, but they may or may not be related. Your brain will relish the freedom to feel without each emotion getting swiftly shuttled into the logical realm. The truth is that you might not care about the milk. You might feel anger from any variety of other sources, including your own memories. This milk incident and your anger may be unrelated. You can't know.

When you are alone on your couch having strong emotions, where do those come from? It's hard to say. You can have old festering emotions that come up in their own time. You might have a mind clouded by conflict that allows you to catch and hold onto emotions that you picked up earlier in the day or week from another person. You might have direct beliefs about emotions that make it hard for you to feel them as they are.

Giving meaning to emotions causes you hold onto them. Your ACC screams, *Do something!* There's nothing to do about an emotion accept to feel it. When you want to do something more with an emotion, that desire causes you to hold on to the emotion like a shipwrecked sailor holding onto a bit of driftwood. When you believe that emotions require actions, you can't let an emotion go until you discover the meaning of it and enact the right *Do something!* response. Of course, there is never a meaning to emotion, so the search for meaning becomes futile. You may resort to assigning a meaning to your emotion at random. You might feel like you've assigned a reasonable meaning to your emotions, but how can you? The vast sources of emotions are too complex for you to definitively know where an emotion came from.

Emotions don't require actions. However, to act on a decision, you will have to use your emotions. Emotion is fundamental and necessary for the act of making a decision. You need emotion to buy a house, choose a turkey sandwich over ham, or to decide where you want to work next. Your logical mind can lay out all of your options, but it can't actually choose. Logic is able to account for the various positives and negatives between options, but a purely logical mind cannot lend a weight to the positives and negatives.[18] In choosing between the purchase of two houses, the logical mind can create an attributes list. House A has a great school system, but it's more expensive, it has a newer roof, the landscaping needs work and the plumbing is old, but the neighbors are fun. Which of those positives outweigh the negatives? The emotional mind fills in the details. You are easily able to see that plumbing and landscaping are less important to you than a bad school system and evil neighbors. That's your emotion channel calling the shots. Your logic or thinking channel would keep doing the math forever.

### Exercise: Taboo Feelings

Families each have their own rules about which emotions are acceptable and which are taboo. These rules are not laws of nature. They are simply cultural guidelines that the family has adopted. When you live or work closely with people from different families who have different rules about emotions, you'll find that conflicts arise over what constitutes acceptable behavior.

To begin: Talk to your parents about which emotions they believe are acceptable and which they believe are taboo. When can emotions be expressed? When is it inappropriate to express emotions? Then talk to someone outside your family and ask the same questions. How are their answers the same? How are they different?

Why it works: All of the emotions are normal. There are no bad ones or dangerous ones. However, cultural rules tend to stigmatize one or more emotions, which then encourages the people in that community to tamp down on hide the taboo emotion or emotions. Stifled emotions will always find a way to express themselves. When an emotion has been stifled for a long time, the expression of that emotion will not be graceful. The emotional explosions that

---

[18] For a short video interview with Antonio Damasio, the neuroscientist who studies how people use emotion to make decisions, search for - When Emotions Make Better Decisions: Antonio Damasio

occur in that community tend to reinforce the belief that the emotion itself is bad and should remain taboo.

Pitfalls: When you spend time with someone who freely expresses an emotion that you believe is taboo, you might come to see that person as breaking a rule. In fact, the rule is your private rule that you share with your family. How is anyone else supposed to even know that the rule exists?

---

# Thought

Descartes wrote, *I think therefore I am*. His true intentions for this statement are lost to time, but each person alive today can ascribe their own meaning. Many think that he was saying that our existence is dependent on our thoughts. His statement, originally in Latin was actually *dubito, ergo cogito, ergo sum* meaning I doubt, therefore I think, therefore I am and suggested that his ability to question his own thoughts was proof that he had thoughts, which was proof that there was some thinking entity in the first place.

Along with Descartes, western philosophy grabbed ahold of thinking as the source of truth and self. However, the idea that truth is best found through thinking is laughable. Thinking is responsible for imagination, lies, pretense, denial, fiction, and illusion. Thinking is just as capable of fabricating falsehood as it is of recognizing truth.

Lie detector machines, polygraphs, have been the standard technology to separate truth from fiction since 1936 when they were first used in a criminal case. The polygraph measures a variety of physiological data while a subject answers questions verbally. Changes in emotional arousal and physiology alerts the test examiner to potential lies. Notice that the best technology we have for separating truth from fiction finds the truth in emotion and physiology. The lies are found in the words.

We have thoughts arising all day long. If you believe that your thoughts are true, you can struggle through a lot of conflict. Most of the chatter in the inner voice is fiction. "That person doesn't like me; don't go down that street because it's dangerous; that is a reasonable price for a coffee; that person is smart; that person is dumb; I could never do what they are doing; I'd be happy if I had the same things as that person; I don't have enough time; I'll be ok as long as I make more money." None of these thoughts are truth. They are the fantastical stories that your mind makes up.

Thinking is unstoppable. Thoughts arise from your beliefs, from memories, from judgments about what you experience, and from other people. Some thoughts make sense and some are nonsense. Some thoughts feel good, others feel bad. The good feeling thoughts are the ones that jive with what you believe and the bad feeling thoughts trigger conflicts. Some thoughts are neutral. They don't have feelings attached to them at all. Oh look! A plane.

Neutral thinking is what happens when you notice a thought and stop there. Just notice it. Often we do more than that. We give thoughts weight by believing that they are true. "You said I was stupid! So, you must think I'm stupid." We attach feelings to them. "I'm angry because you drank all the milk." Or we decide on actions that must be taken when the ACC screams *Do something!* "If you don't apologize right now, I'm going to find a way to punish you."

All thoughts can be neutral. No matter what the thought is referencing in real life, you can watch it from a neutral position. When thoughts pop up in your mind, you don't have to give them weight. "I left the door unlocked." "Our child got into a fight today." "You disappointed me." These are all just thoughts. Even if you find a thought that is already attached to a feeling, "Your behavior makes me so mad," you can look at *that* with neutrality. It's a thought. It's just as likely to be false as it is to be true. Thoughts are not to be trusted!

Even your ideas about yourself are thoughts. You may have a strong sense of your identity. You may feel like you know exactly who you are, but how can you be sure that your idea of yourself is not just a thought? Do you need those thoughts about yourself so that you exist? Or is your continued existence possible even as your thoughts about yourself shift and change?

Other people can share their thoughts with you through language. You might be able to follow them, or you might not. Even when you try to listen, you might find your mind wandering. You might focus and unfocus multiple times in the same conversation. Sometimes you can hear the meaning intended by your conversation partner, but not always.

Distracted listening is done through thoughts and logic, without the benefit of the other channels. You can't fully listen to someone using only your thought channel. The thought channel is noisy on it's own and there's a lot of interference from your own thoughts. They constantly pop in to ask you if you are listening, if you left your phone in the car, or what's on your calendar next. You can't even be sure you are listening. Your thoughts can trick you into thinking you were. Thoughts are wily.

## Using MindSET to Find Truth

Although we lend a lot of credence to thinking, it's not a very trustworthy channel of information. Thinking is prone to fabrication which means the information that you get through your thought channel is just as often fiction as it is true. Emotions are always true, however, they have no meaning. Emotions can come from anyone and anywhere so you can't attribute reason to an emotion. Sensations are ever present, but they can't be translated into logical meanings either. It may seem like a highly challenging endeavor to listen to the world using your three channels of MindSET. You've got unreliable logic, meaningless truth, and more meaningless truth. How do you make use of that?

When you use all three channels together they work better than the sum of the parts. Together, the channels have strengths that you can use to find truth. To use MindSET, you anchor yourself to truth through whatever you are currently feeling without applying any reasons or judgments. Then, you see what thoughts arise. You are more likely to discover true thoughts if you are already anchored in the truth of your feelings. False thoughts will come too. As you open yourself to experiencing all three channels at once, you will find that you are able to be present and listen. If you feel yourself slipping into reaction, or allowing your mind to wander during a conversation, you can connect to your sensations and emotions and they will bring you back into the present.

Imagine a conversation with a coworker over lunch. You meet up, order food, and get to talking. Your coworker shares a string of information through words. You hear a story about something that is going on with management that might trigger a shift in departments. Jobs might be at stake. He tells you that you should probably start looking for a new job. Do you believe him? Should you be worried? What do you do here?

To use MindSET, you can check in with your emotions to center yourself in truth. You may find that you came into the conversation from a logical perspective and emotion might be hard to access at first. Instead, you can look to sensation to find truth and presence. Your palms are a little sweaty and your heart is beating faster than normal. Those observations are truth. Then you notice that you are scared. You thought you were hesitant (a form of fear) to try this new process of using MindSET in real life, but maybe you are feeling scared because scared is the predominant emotion at the table. You test the truth in that emotion, by responding to the conversation. Your lunch mate just told you some details about a memo he intercepted. "Scary," you say. Your lunch mate agrees and keeps talking. Ah confirmation, you felt fear and he felt fear. You are experiencing truth.

Once you anchor yourself in truth, it's much easier to listen to information coming through in thoughts. It's almost like thoughts get color coded by truth and fiction once you anchor yourself in your feelings. Thoughts get color coded in other ways too. Your lunch mate gives you some line about how the company is always growing, and you can see that it's color coded as though it was coming directly out of his boss's mouth, not his mouth. "That's Joe's line," you quip. He agrees.

The food comes and you notice that your drink isn't filled to the top. A thought arises in your mind, "They are cheating me!" But you know better. It's not the restaurant that's cheating you, your lunch mate feels cheated by the company. All the words he's saying are about retirement investments and college funds, but the feeling that just came up in you is about being cheated. You check in with him, "I don't know about you, but I feel cheated." He responds, "Tell me about it! We deserve to be treated better."

As you wrap up lunch, you realize that you have talked about a lot of thoughts with your lunch mate, but a few points stood out as deep truth. He is afraid of being cheated. The stuff about retirement funds and other surface ideas were about having a polite discussion. Those statements were bolstering beliefs. He wanted solidarity. He wanted to feel seen and heard.

If you were paying attention only to the thoughts in the conversation, you might be freaked out after that lunch. You might be focused on your finances and you'd have an underlying sense of fear that you couldn't shake. You'd be likely to decide that your company is going under, your finances are at risk and you need to *Do something!* But that isn't the truth. The truth is that your lunch mate found a memo and he's scared about being cheated. That's all. Fortunately, you know how to use MindSET so you can listen to more than the thought channel.

MindSET works because each of the channels provide a different kind of information. Thoughts are made of logic and because of the nature of logic, you can have both true and false logic. Information on the thought channel could be true or false; you can't know when you use thoughts alone, because there's no anchor to truth. You can anchor yourself in truth if you can find an emotion. Emotion is made of something that either exists or does not. There's no such thing as false emotion. Someone can pretend to have an emotion, but you won't feel it through empathy. As we looked at in a previous chapter, mirror neurons only respond to true emotion, not mimicked emotion. Actors know this implicitly; they can't fake it or the audience won't feel it.

Sensation is helpful when emotion is very strong or very weak. Strong emotion can push you into reaction. You might discover a fiery anger inside that shuts you down and puts you in reaction. If that happens, you can't listen at all. On the other end of the spectrum, you might find that you can't feel an emotion. You look, and there's nothing there. In both cases, you can fall back on bodily sensations. You can always feel the ground under your feet, the clothes on your body, and the air going in and out through your breath. Sensation doesn't give you information about the emotional states of those around you, but it's still a good way to find truth.

Staying connected to truth through emotion and sensation, you can navigate thoughts easily. You can start to see where you've been fooling yourself. You can see where others are fooling themselves. You can know how people feel although you can never know why they feel that way. You can see what scares you about your memories. There's a lot of information in the truth. Being able to separate truth from fiction is a hugely valuable skill.

# The Trouble with Feelings

To get to truth, you must be willing to feel. To find and let go of beliefs you have to be willing to feel the emotions that are connected to events and memories of the past. For many, this is a problem. Feelings are written off as intense, unpleasant, and signs of weakness instead of recognized as normal, healthy, and important to an individual's connection with the world. If you have been downplaying emotion in your life, then you may have an extra hurdle to overcome. Those who have been unwilling to feel emotion have developed tricks to avoid emotion at all costs. Some even learn to pretend they are having emotions by guessing which emotion would be appropriate and claiming that it's happening. Faking an emotion is not the same as having an emotion. It's like pretending to eat. You get none of the benefits.

Everyone has emotions.[19] You can't stop emotions from happening, but you can disconnect yourself from them so you don't recognize them anymore. You can also go into reaction the second an emotion starts happening. If you tend to get overwhelmed with emotion, every time you try to use MindSET to find truth you'll end up in reaction. Some people shut down emotionally in reaction; you might find that you pop into your happy place where and pretend that you didn't feel anything. If you struggle with emotions, then go ahead and forget about them for a while. Start with sensations and deeply explore the feelings of your body throughout the day. Tickles, pressures, belly grumbles, notice everything you feel and take nothing for granted. This will help calibrate your *Do something!* threshold so that you can start to experience emotion without going into reaction.

Most people have one or more emotions that they prefer not to experience or express. Families teach children beliefs about emotions. In some families it's not ok to express sadness, frustration, or anger. In

---

[19] The Dalai Lama and psychologist Paul Ekman collaborated to create an online atlas of the universal human emotions. You can find this by searching for: Atlas of Emotion.

other families, it's not ok to express joy. What are your emotional patterns? What beliefs do you have about emotions?

---

## Exercise: Expressing All the Emotions

Most people have trouble expressing one or more of the basic human emotions. This often comes as a surprise. Unless you have trained in acting or voice work, you probably haven't had an occasion to test whether you can express all of the emotions.

The universal human emotions are: Fear, sadness, anger, disgust, and enjoyment. There are varying degrees of each as listed below.

Enjoyment: amusement, pride, excitement
Sadness: disappointment, helplessness, sorrow
Disgust: dislike, repugnance, loathing
Fear: nervousness, desperation, terror
Anger: annoyance, bitterness, fury

To begin: Find a group of people 3 or more who are willing to do this exercise with you.

You will say a line, "Put the buttons back in the jar." You will attempt to convey an emotion by saying only that line.

For example, I might try to get my group to feel the emotion disgust. I would conjure up the feeling of eating a bug or finding a hair in my food, then I would say the line. My teammates will sense disgust if I'm expressing it. Repeat with all of the emotions. Can your teammates guess correctly? Whatever they receive from you, that's what you are expressing. Use your audience as a judge.

Why this works: If you discover that you have trouble bringing an emotion to the surface so that you can express it, it's likely that you've been stifling that emotion for a long time. You no longer have control over that emotion.

Pitfalls: When you find an emotion you can't express clearly, think about your relationship to that emotion. Do you believe that it's ok to have that emotion? Notice how your life might be affected by stifling, and therefore having a lack of control over, that emotion.

Feeling emotions is a bit like eating food. You are familiar with the process of eating food. Food goes in, gets processed, and about a day later, it passes through. You get benefits from the food in terms of pleasure and nutrients, and the rest comes out as waste. If you don't pass the waste, then a backup begins to occur. Any new food that goes in, can't come back out. The food related term for this is constipation. Emotions are similar.

You receive emotions from the world around you, you process them, and they pass through you. Instead of a digestive tract, you can picture each person's emotional processing equipment like a mesh netting. Emotions come in through the net and past out. Normally, feeling an emotion gives you the emotional benefits of empathy and the pleasure of connecting with those around you, then the emotion keeps moving out of the net. If at some point, you chose to ignore an emotion, to not notice it, then that emotion gets stuck to the net. Over time, you may have gotten into a habit of not noticing emotions, maybe you were never taught how to notice emotions, and they all became glued to the net. Now, each emotion that you feel gets stuck in the net just because there's no possible way anything can pass through. It's emotional constipation. Every emotion feels intense and horrible just like a sandwich would make you feel intense and horrible if your intestines were blocked.

There's a lot of misunderstanding about how emotions work, and most people find ways to cope on their own. Someone probably taught you a healthy way to eat and eliminate your waste, but you might not have gotten a similar lesson about emotions. It's a fundamental practice, and it's overlooked, probably because the people who raised you didn't know how to do it either. We take for granted how important it is to learn healthy fecal elimination practices because we tend to do a good job of it in the developed world. In some parts of the world, there are rampant chronic diseases like parasites and intestinal disorders because of unhealthy elimination practices. The developed world has learned how to standardize the practices of passing waste and washing up safely, but we have not learned how to process emotions. Instead of parasites, we suffer from anger management issues, depression, anxiety, and attention disorders. The whole thing has become a mess.

At first, you might struggle to feel any emotion at all. Perhaps you hid that emotion net away so well, you forgot where you put it. When you find it, you might be overwhelmed with what you find. It might be a big mess. You might act out, have a few verbal outbursts, or find yourself in tears in a bathroom somewhere. This is ok, and well worth the interim unpleasantries. Unexpected and intense emotions are temporary. Your experience will change when you clear the net of festering emotions. Emotions are unruly only because you've been emotionally constipated for a long time. After you get through all of the junk stuck in your net, you can have graceful emotional experiences. Once the net is clear, you feel emotions without being compelled in any way. There's no need to speak, or act. You can just feel.

Imagine your fortress of beliefs again for a moment. The tower in the middle contains your ideal life. It's surrounded by walls made of beliefs. One of those walls, on the outside edge close to where you are standing, is a wall that is made of all your rules about how to deal with emotions and other feelings. You have rules about what is rude and what is polite. How to treat the elderly and people who have authority. You have rules about what you can and cannot say to other people's children or other people's spouses. Your rules are not the same as everyone else's. You developed these rules and built this wall in hopes of connecting with people and being a good person. This wall is meant to bring you closer to others. You hoped it would help you follow social expectations and act in a way that others could enjoy you or at least tolerate you. Unfortunately, that wall is blocking you from getting to truth. It's blocking you from your ideal life and it's also preventing you from connecting with others unconditionally.

The beliefs you have about emotions and social rules came from your childhood. You either followed the rules that your family taught you, or you came up with your own strategies. Those beliefs are now yours and you are the only one who can change them or let them go. It's ok, you can unlearn those strategies and process emotion through noticing, but first, you need to recognize your beliefs about emotions.

Beliefs about emotions are just like beliefs about anything else. They cause conflicts just like any other beliefs. However, beliefs about emotions are necessary to address before you can dig into your other beliefs. You need to be able to experience emotion so that you can dive deeply into all your beliefs. When you embark on your hero's journey in search of your key beliefs, you will be following your feelings, not your thoughts. Sensations and emotions are the breadcrumbs that lead you to the keystone in your fortress wall.

---

## Exercise: Beliefs About Emotion

The following is a non-exhaustive list of the beliefs that some people hold about emotions.

To begin: Read through and see if any of these beliefs ring true for you. Copy the ones you can relate to in your journal. Do you have a belief that isn't on this list? Record your own beliefs about emotions.

Emotions are a sign of weakness.
Crying is a sign of weakness.
Losing your temper is a sign of weakness.
Emotions are only for women (men, children, poor people, the uneducated, etc)
Emotional people are not logical.
Emotional people are not powerful.
Personalities are either logical or emotional.
Smart people are logical, not emotional.
Emotions are dangerous, (distracting, bothersome, uncomfortable, painful).
Feelings have meaning.
It's important to do what feels good, right, etc.
Feeling bad means something bad is happening.
It's ok to cry only when someone dies.
My emotions are my fault (or your fault, his fault, her fault)
I want to be happy all the time.
It's possible to be happy all the time.
I never learned how to have feelings so it's too late.
When I have feelings dangerous (scary, extreme, embarrassing) things happen.
I can be possessed by my emotions.
It's important to hide your emotions from others.
It's important to act as soon as you feel bad so that you can start feeling better.
It's my job to make people happy when I love them.
Joy (sadness, anger, disgust, fear) is a private emotion.
It's my job to bring joy to others.
Emotions like (anger, sadness, joy, etc) show that you care.
I have to hide my emotions to protect others

Why it works: Your beliefs are so fundamental to you that you often can't put them into words. Identifying your beliefs allows you to determine whether you actually agree with them.

Pitfalls: When you discover you have a belief about emotion and you disagree with it, you might struggle to simply drop that belief. To get rid of a belief, explore the feelings that you have associate with it. Once you feel through the belief, you can drop it.

---

# Conditional Truths

Beliefs are not truth, but it can be hard to know what is the truth, especially when you have lived with certain beliefs your whole life. Your beliefs about emotion might seem like a law of nature. How can you be sure what is truth and what is a belief? Connecting with sensation and emotion, in other words, using MindSET, is one way to get on the same page with truth. There are a few other things you can look at as you examine your beliefs to see what's true and what's made up.

Truth is the same as a law of nature. Gravity is always true. Even if you leave the planet, gravitational fields still exist. The pull becomes smaller as two objects move apart. Gravitational fields don't turn on and off. They work on all bodies equally based on mass. Truths are true for everyone.

Beliefs are less likely to be true all the time. When something is true sometimes and false other times it's conditional. Under one condition it's true, and under another condition it's false. An example belief from the list above is that smart people are logical, not emotional. How can you explain a smart person who cries when they are moved? Does IQ go down while a person cries? To qualify the beliefs, you might argue that most smart people are logical, but there might be a few people who can be both logical and emotional. See? You can start to see the conditionality of this belief. It affects some people and not others. It's not uniform for everyone.

Another example of a conditional belief is the notion of rude behavior. What does it mean to be rude? Does it mean the same thing in the United

States as it does in China? Is it rude to make noise with your mouth while you eat? In San Francisco, yes, but in Shanghai, no. And so it must be a conditional rule and therefore a belief, not a law of nature.

What about this statement? Is it true? *Life includes death.* Death occurs to all living things. It doesn't matter who you are or where you are, your body will die at some point. Death is then, a law of nature, like gravity. Laws of nature will always be true, no matter where you grew up, or how old you are. Laws of nature are the same for all people no matter when you are alive. Even those who argue for eternal life admit that the body dies.

When you discover some of your beliefs about emotion, test them out on other people. Ask if they believe the same thing. Beliefs, can be contested between people. Beliefs are opinions, generally conditional, and they are learned from our families and our experience.

Another good hint that you are dealing with a belief is if you find yourself defending it. The truth is the truth. There is no defense needed. If no one comes to the rescue of the truth, it will go on existing without anyone's help. Beliefs, and the walls they make up, require their owners to defend them or they might begin to crumble. The next time you find yourself defending the way you were raised, the ways of your people, or why you are the way you are, notice that there might be a belief you are trying to protect.

Your head may be spinning from confusion about what is true and what is belief. The rules of everyday life are mostly beliefs. Here are a few of the truths.

- Two competing beliefs create conflict.
- Conflict is uncomfortable.
- Uncertainty is uncomfortable.
- Pretending (without being clear that you are pretending) leads to suffering.
- Acting without integrity leads to suffering.
- Thoughts are made of logic, which can be either true or false.
- Beliefs are thoughts.
- People can share emotions without language.
- Life includes death.

# Let It Go

You now know where beliefs come from (community, family, and experience), how they cause trouble (conflict), and what can happen if you don't manage them (suffering). You might be eager and ready to let go of some beliefs, and still a bit unsure of how to proceed. The time has come. You now have enough information to start your hero's journey.

There are phases to letting a belief go. First, you'll notice some part of the problem, either through chronic suffering or acute conflict. Usually, this will seem like you are in direct opposition to someone else. You will identify some or all of the people (dead or alive) who are involved. By connecting to your MindSET and anchoring to truth, you will be able to shift your perspective and with that mental agility, you will discover what role you play in the problem. You will be able to access new emotions which allow you to dive deeper into the perspective shift, so you can see the problem from many angles.

Remember that the Zeigarnik Effect is an exacerbation of the feeling of conflict that comes from having open circles. Check to see how you are missing some elements of integrity and you can close some circles for instant conflict relief. Also, you will find thoughts in your mind that accuse others of bad behavior. Check to see if you might be exhibiting that bad behavior too. Often we see in others the things we dislike about ourselves. You can find more emotions and dive deeper over and over until you get to a clear articulation or understanding of the belief. After you find the belief, and feel through the emotions attached to it, you can decide to let it go or keep it.

**Phases of letting go of a belief**

1. At first, the problem looks like it's being caused by someone else.
2. Perspective shift allows you to see how you have a responsibility in perpetuating (but not for causing) the conflict. Do not assign blame to yourself or anyone else.

3. Connect deeply to any emotions and sensations you feel without creating reasons for your feelings.

4. Notice your thoughts without trying to determine which are true and which are false.

5. Eventually, you'll notice that some thoughts seem to be connected to strong feelings. Explore those thoughts. They might be beliefs.

6. When you find yourself feeling like someone else is causing your problem, go back to the beginning and repeat the steps. It might take many iterations to find the belief.

**Double check**

- Check to see how your behavior is not in integrity. Do you have any open circles? Open circles can make conflict feel much bigger than it would be if you closed those circles.

- Often we accuse others of exhibiting the bad behavior that we are exhibiting ourselves. It's easier to see it when someone else does it. Check to see if you are disappointed with your own behavior or performance.

It's important to remember that logic isn't a prominent part of letting go of beliefs. The beliefs came from old feelings that were processed into logic. Using too much logic tends to keep the beliefs secure in their wall. Stay anchored to the truth of your emotions and let logic swing between truth and fiction as you navigate your thoughts. Memories can be fantastical and just plain wrong. That's ok.

To help you see how letting go works in real life, here is a case study of a man, we'll call Val, who let go of a key belief during the writing of this book. Val was suffering. He was working feverishly on research for a new product he was trying to develop. He was working as a professor and he lived with his wife and young son. He found himself sick in bed for a week even though it was summer time, not flu season. He knew he was working himself too hard. He couldn't take the suffering anymore, but he didn't know how to stop.

I asked Val what the problem was. He had a nagging internal voice that kept asking "Are you sure you aren't the wrong person?" He said that he was feverishly working on research for his new product. He was trying to become the CEO of his own new company and kept having doubts about whether he was the right person for the role. Also, in spending his time starting a company, he was missing out on spending time with his child and wife. He was afraid that if he slowed down on the research, that he would lose the investment that he put into the company. The money was significant, and he admitted that it would take a few years to replenish the savings. Val started developing the product because he hoped that it would save people. His technology is something you might use in the ICU of a hospital. Like many entrepreneurs, Val was driven by a compulsion to save the world in his own small way.

Ideally, Val would see that it was possible to balance his time between family, work, and his research. His wife made a good salary. He could keep working on his product on the side, little by little. He could stay in integrity with his own family values by devoting a bit more time to his family and less time to the new product he was developing, which was, by his own admission, a side project.

The problem really was that Val was torn between being a good dad and saving the world. He was aware of his deep need to save the world and he shared the details with me. As a child he fantasized about growing up to be Batman. He had a rough childhood and he survived it. He wore that adversity like a badge of honor. He had emancipated himself as a teen so he could get an education. His childhood abuse felt to him like something that helped him be strong. It helped him be who he was. His adversity gave him strength, but it also kept him down. Every belief has a dark side and a light side. He felt as though he could take on the world, but he was also plagued with an inner voice that constantly told him that he wasn't smart enough. That was the voice of his abuser.

Val is an engineer, an intellectual, and a professor. He experienced a lot of therapy as an adult, so he was well aware of the difference between the intellectual and the emotional. He knew how to access all three channels of MindSET. His ability to purposefully connect with his feelings made it much easier for him to let go of his belief. We talked one day, when he was particularly distraught over his own time management. With a little prodding, he was able to shift his perspective. He saw how it could be possible for him to manage his time so that he would be able to work on his company and be present for his family. The limitation of time was a bolstering belief distracting him from the deeper, less polite conversation topic. He saw that it wasn't time that was the problem. It was his compulsion to save the world that was the problem. When Val felt some combination of emotions well up inside him he didn't consciously notice them. Instead his ACC processed those emotions into *Do something!* and he dutifully drove to the lab in response to do more research. When Val was in reaction, he dove into his work.

Val looked into his problems with the intention of shifting his perspective. He asked himself, what can I see differently here? It didn't take long before he saw his belief from a different angle. He realized that his compulsion to save the world was wrapped up with that voice that told him he wasn't smart enough and the other voice that kept questioning whether he was the right person. Although he thought that his mind was telling him he was the wrong person to run the company, he was misinterpreting that voice. The message wasn't about his company. When Val connected to his emotions, he was able to see the message with less attached meaning, "Are you sure you aren't the wrong person?" What else could that mean?

How else might he have interpreted that message. He ran through ideas. It might mean, he's the wrong person for the company. It might mean that he's the wrong person for his classroom of students. Maybe he's the wrong person for his family. When he started to think about his family, his emotions swelled. Instantly, he knew what the message meant. His mind was telling him that he wasn't behaving as the person he wanted to be, the attentive dad and husband. Instead he kept heeding his ACC and chasing his compulsion to go work in the lab. It was a simple integrity problem that was staring him in the face. He wasn't following his own values. The insight about his nagging internal voice was fundamental, but it wasn't enough to help him let go of the key belief supporting his troubles. He still felt driven to run to the lab when he felt overwhelmed.

Val's belief was that he was shaped into who he is by his early childhood abuse. He used the adversity like a badge of honor so that he could get through hard times, but he suspected that it was driving his compulsion to save the world. He decided that, rather than waking up with a compulsion to run to the lab every morning, that he would prefer to wake up and have a real choice about how he might spend his day. He wanted to be able to hang out with his young son without compulsively thinking about his research. He wanted to be present for his family and this desire drove him to let go of the belief. He told me over the phone, "I'm standing here in the lab right now holding a rubber glove. If my belief were a glove, I could let it go. I could throw it away out of my life, but it's not a tangible thing. How do I get to this belief? How do I then let it go?" I was happy he asked.

I reminded him that beliefs are formed when we don't fully process emotions. Although Val told me that he suffered abuse as a child, there was no need for him to share the details with me. I didn't ask. He simply needed to feel the emotions that were connected to his desire to save the world. To get to the belief in the present, he had to be willing to feel the things that were attached to that belief. I reminded him that the feelings he had in the present would not be necessarily the feelings that happened in the past. He might feel any range of emotions and whatever he felt was ok. All he had to do was notice the feelings. He excused himself from the phone and later told me that he felt the wave of emotion building. He felt the urge to devote himself to noticing immediately.

Val discovered that using his adversity like a badge of honor had caused him more trouble than he originally knew. As he felt through the emotions that were rising for him, he realized there was a lot of anger and resentment. It was a surprise to him that those feelings weren't connected to his childhood abuse at all. His feelings were connected to recent events and relationships. Val said that using his abuse as a badge of honor masked recent adversity he experienced. Put another way, Val would not have chosen to put himself through recent difficult events if he had not been so eager to use his badge of honor to prove that he could handle it. His belief, that his childhood adversity made him impervious to pain, caused him to race towards and suffer through events and relationships that another person would have eagerly avoided. Once he saw the false logic in his belief and saw how it indirectly hurt his family by triggering compulsions to run off to do research, he was able to toss that belief like an empty can.

## Belief Retirement Recap

Val was able to identify something in his life that wasn't working for him. This can be a conflict, fight, compulsion, or just a lingering sense that something needs to change. People can start to notice a malaise settle over themselves as they realize that they've been suffering for quite some time. Val had been suffering, but it was a week in bed that finally made him sit up and take notice.

People usually have some preoccupation and/or compulsion that accompanies their suffering. Val was preoccupied with his time management. That's what was on his mind on a daily basis. His drive to spend his time wisely was underwritten by a compulsion to save the world (and to prove himself smart in the process). That compulsion competed with what he said he would do as a dad, spend time with his child. He was acting outside of integrity by not matching his actions with his own values.

There were a few pivotal points for Val. His ability to shift his perspective was crucial. He might have gotten stuck in denial. He might have been unable to see that he didn't need to be in the lab. He might have gone further to say that he had a fundraising issue and that if he had a million dollars, he could work full time on this project and get it done faster. Fortunately for Val, he didn't defend his problem. He didn't use denial. Val was open minded about his perspectives. He was ready to shift and bob and weave through the true and false logic in his mind. His perspective shift was triggered by me asking, "Are you sure you are not the wrong person?" which was his question to himself. He saw the answer immediately. He wasn't spending his time the way he thought he should be. He wasn't being the person he wanted to be. When you look for chances to shift your perspective, you can focus on things you wrote in your journal that stood out to you. Ask other people to read your sentences out of context. What else might it mean? What are your uncontrolled thoughts trying to tell you?

To let go of his belief, Val had to be willing to feel whatever emotions were attached to his belief. He was willing, and it wasn't pretty, but he noticed everything he could through an intense emotional rollercoaster. Even days later he felt wrung out. It might sound like Val is a pro at letting go of beliefs, but I'm not telling you the whole story. About a month prior to Val's belief retirement, he spent a good ten minutes explaining to me how he was going to replace his belief with a better version. He was mentally crafting a new belief that could take the place of his Batman Saves the World Belief. I looked at him and asked, "Are you negotiating?" He got my drift. That comment was a nod to Elizabeth

Kübler-Ross' highly criticized five stages of grief. One of the stages people tend to go through when they are learning to accept a big change is negotiation. So, Val had been planning the retirement of his belief for a while, at least a month. I don't want to read too much into his experience, but Kübler-Ross' would have pointed to his week-long bed stay as the depression part of letting go. All that was left was for him to feel the emotions and come to acceptance.

I tell this story partly because it happened while I was writing this chapter, so it was fresh on my mind, but also because it's the story of a very serious childhood wound that might initially seem impossible to heal. The abuse that Val suffered as a child was untenable. Some people have very bad luck and experience something horrible, but those wounds don't damage a person permanently. Hurt people aren't damaged or defective. They can let go of beliefs just like people who have not suffered atrocities. Val's success was owed to his ability to see that he could still be a strong person without his protective key belief. He saw that he could chose his actions without being driven by his compulsion. It was like Dumbo's feather all over again. Val could be himself, and he didn't need his childhood belief that he was Batman anymore to do so. Now, without the belief, Val can be Batman one day and devoted dad the next day, whatever he chooses to do. He's no longer compelled to run to the lab when he'd rather just be dad.

This example was a belief that came from childhood abuse. Other people will have beliefs that might have come from perfectly happy childhoods. Beliefs are painful, not necessarily because the initial cause was unjust. Some people report that they feel ridiculous that they didn't get their beliefs sorted out years ago. Imagine a belief that comes from a misunderstanding when a person was a small child. A simple misunderstanding can create beliefs that ruin marriages decades later. Other beliefs are the kind that start as a small lie that gets bigger and bigger the longer it goes on. Some beliefs come from good intentions, not just abuse. Beliefs cause trouble in the present. Letting go of beliefs allows the past to be past and the present to be present.

## Summary of Key Concepts

- Memories are fallible, changeable, and not reliable.

- Emotion has no owner, no definitive source and no reasons for existing. Empathy works by feeling only. Thinking gets in the way of empathy.

- Truths are laws of nature, which are different than beliefs or opinions.

- Thoughts are made of logic which can be true or false.

- Beliefs came from hastily tidied feelings, so to let go of beliefs, you have to feel the feelings that are still connected to the belief.

- Thinking is unstoppable. Neutral thinking is what happens when you notice a thought and stop there without trying to decide whether it's true or false.

- Distracted listening is done through thoughts and logic, without the benefit of the other channels. You can't fully listen to someone using only your thought channel.

- Thinking is prone to fabrication which means the information that you get through your thought channel is just as often fiction as it is true. Emotions are always true, however, they have no meaning. Sensations are ever present, but they can't be translated into logical meanings either.

- Emotional constipation causes emotions to feel intense and painful. While clearing your net, unexpected and intense emotions are temporary. Once the net is clear, you feel emotions without being compelled in any way. There's no need to speak, or act. You can just feel.

- When you look for beliefs and get ready to let them go, you will be following your feelings, not your thoughts. Sensations and emotions are the bread crumbs that you follow to get to the heart of what's going.

# 7: Retiring Key Beliefs

*The truth does not change according to our ability to stomach it.*

Flannery O'Connor

Many of life's problems can be traced to a mismatch between the way you think the world works, and your experience of how the world actually works. When those two things don't match up, you have a conflict. Most relationship problems, whether romantic, work-related, family, or friend, are caused directly by this mismatch between beliefs and experience. Beliefs affect your relationship to non-sentient things too. Your relationships with food, love, money, religion, sex, and anything else you can think of are directly affected by your beliefs. Cravings, habits, and addictions all rely on your beliefs so that they can exist in your life. Your beliefs stand like the walls of your fortress preventing you from living the life you want.

You now know all the elements needed to diminish conflict in your life. You have the formula. The physical, logical, and emotional work together to allow you to shift your perspective and see how your beliefs aren't laws of nature. With that mystery solved, you are likely ready to get on with it and end some conflicts of your own.

Life is different after you find your key beliefs and retire them. You can focus and be present, even when you are in a boring situation; you can pay attention and listen to the nuances of what's going on in the room. You can respect and listen to others even when they have wildly different views from your own. You'll be able to see how you habitually lie to yourself and others, and you'll see how most everyone else does too. The polite complaints of the bolstering beliefs that people share publicly will become obvious to you. The direct connection between your decisions and life's path will emerge clearly. Some things are forever at the mercy of chance, but you'll have more control over your life's outcomes than you ever knew was possible. You will be better able to see how living in integrity keeps conflict from creeping into your life. Most of all, you will feel better mentally and physically, you'll be less stressed, and less torn between competing decisions.

## Step 1: Conflict

First you have to notice that you are having a conflict. Conflicts initially look like they are caused by someone else. Conflicts come with intense feelings and you may find yourself compelled to act in a specific way. There might be a fight, or you might avoid a confrontation, either way, you are in a conflict. In some cases, the conflict can be subtle. You may find yourself denying that you have any real problems. Your first hurdle is to get from denial of the problem to a recognition that there is a problem.

## Step 2: Perspective shift

Finding your beliefs means questioning your own reality. It requires a shift in perspective that can be jarring at first. This chapter shares true stories about people discovering and letting go of their beliefs so that they can live with less conflict. In each story look for the initial perspective shift that allowed them to see things differently. Sometimes the shift is subtle. Often it occurs, not by trying hard and pushing yourself to see something new, but by relaxing into the possibility that your perspective may not be the truth. Also notice how it's possible for a person to get stuck by holding their own perspective stubbornly. Counter to intuition, chastising yourself for being stubborn isn't the solution. Defending your stubbornness isn't a solution either. Instead, notice your adherence to your perspective and be open to any window of opportunity to see things a new way, whenever and however that might occur.

## Step 3: Feel for truth

Once you gain some insight into new perspectives about your beliefs, you may feel elated and excited that you were able to see things differently. It's spectacular progress, but it's not the finish line. The beliefs you initially discover will be bolstering beliefs. They are the beliefs that support the walls of your fortress. The key beliefs will be well hidden under layers of feelings. To get to the key belief, you will have to use the trifecta of MindSET tools that you have learned in previous chapters so that you can anchor to the truth of feelings and explore your thoughts as they swing wildly between true and false.

**Tool One (physical):** You will calibrate your ACC so that you are less sensitive to going into reaction. Calibrating your brain is a physical activity that works like exercise. If you do the exercise, it works. If you pretend to do the exercise, nothing happens. Over just a few weeks of doing daily ACC exercise, you can feel less irritability, less emotional pain, and less physical pain. Many of the ACC exercises focus on noticing sensations.

**Tool Two (emotional):** You will learn to accept and express all of the human emotions, enjoyment, sadness, anger, fear, and disgust. Each emotion eventually dissolves when you notice it, but not when you act it out through hurting another person. Denying that you are having emotions doesn't allow for you to process them. Pushing away one or more specific emotions clogs the emotional net and creates emotional constipation. Remember, emotions aren't logical and don't have reasons or justifications. If you find that you have a good reason to feel a certain way, beware! You might be reasoning your emotions instead of noticing them.

**Tool Three (logical):** You will learn to let your thoughts prattle on without giving them weight. Thoughts can be either true or false and they feel the same either way. You will have more false thoughts than true ones, especially at first. When a thought feels true, don't trust it immediately. Check to see that it has no judgments or decisions attached to it. A true thought is simply a reflection of what is. It can't be argued against. "This ball is blue" is a potentially false thought. "This ball looks blue to me" is a true thought. In the following stories, look to see where each person uses sensations, emotions, and thoughts together to dive deeper into their beliefs.

## Step 3: Integrity maintenance

As you gain clarity of mind, you will be able to see when you are in integrity and when you are not. Integrity is a daily concern like hygiene. You have to pay attention to it and keep up with it regularly. Integrity is not just about following through with the tasks and appointments you said you'd do, it's much more than that. Integrity is about discovering the lies you tell yourself and others so you can stop using false logic in your decision making. It's about being honest about the emotions you feel when you feel them, instead of pretending that you aren't having emotions in the moment. Integrity is also about communicating clearly without ever making assumptions about how you or someone else might think, feel, or behave in the future. Integrity is not a praxis for many people, so adding integrity to your life can be a big change. Integrity always improves lives. You can't go wrong with integrity. When you are experiencing a conflict, there is undoubtedly a crack in your own integrity. In the following stories look for failures in integrity. Look to see how improving integrity helps the person in the story find more clarity.

---

### Exercise: Integrity

Integrity is simply wholeness or completeness. Things that are incomplete tend to get the brain's attention. Even an incomplete circle on paper gets your attention more than a complete circle. When incomplete things in your life get your brain's attention, that's less attention you get to put on the things you want to think about.

To begin: Identify all the ways you are living without integrity. Are you following rules you don't agree with? Are you ignoring values you do believe in? Are you leaving things open ended? Are you dragging your feet about something you've been meaning to do?

Why this works: Life is complicated and there will always be something you've left undone. Making a list can help you identify which items are creating uncontrollable mental activity.

Pitfalls: Don't fret about integrity. If you find that you are worried about integrity or that you get stressed about seeing someone else act with a lack of integrity, then let it go for a while. Keeping an eye on integrity is about decreasing distractions, not creating more. When integrity becomes a distraction, it's no longer helping you.

---

Each story looks at real people who struggled with conflict. Since these are real experiences, they might not follow a formula perfectly. In each story, look for the perspective shift. Look to see how emotion, or lack thereof affects the hunt for beliefs. Look for breaks in integrity. Some of these stories include a person who successfully retired a belief and gained a totally new outlook on life. Other stories show ways that people have gotten stuck in bolstering beliefs, denial, and lack of integrity. None of these stories are finished because all of the people in these stories are still alive and still learning about their beliefs each day. Belief-hunting is a lifelong endeavor. No matter how many you find right now, changes in your life will uncover more through new conflicts.

# Alice's Story: Getting Stuck

Each belief has a life of its own. You can't just go through this process once and eradicate your beliefs. Each belief will have its own feelings associated with it. Even if you have found and retired a few beliefs, it can be tricky to tackle the next one. It gets easier, but only to a point. Finding beliefs is like hunting for anything; even if you know where to look, and you have all the tools, you still have to do the leg work.

Each time you have a conflict, you will start out in a denial phase. Even though you may know logically that the conflict is due to your own beliefs contradicting your experience, it will still feel as though you are being wronged by some other person, people, or force. This is the first step, the phase when you just notice your thoughts as they tell you about the injustice you've suffered.

Your thoughts will conjure ways in which your feelings are justified and your displeasure is condoned. You now know better than to believe those thoughts. Denial is a phase that will pass as you begin to see things from new perspectives. Getting stuck in denial can (and does) happen to everyone at some point. Here's what it looks like when you can't seem to shake the idea that you've done everything perfectly and other people or outside forces are at the root of the problem.

Alice's problem was that she was in debt and had been for many years. She owed about $10k in credit card bills and four times as much in student loans. She lived rent-free in a relative's home when she could no longer afford living on her own. Her troubles were not limited to money problems. She'd gotten into some trouble with the law and was doing probation. The court-ordered psychotherapy and probation visits were hard on her wallet too. She was also fired from her job working a very stable, but low paying position in a large medical facility. She began to fight with the last of her remaining friends and relatives who treated her as an equal. When she was asked to move out of her relative's house, she knew she was coming to the end of her rope. She was homeless, in debt, broke, and on probation.

Ideally, Alice would recognize that she must be out of integrity for things to have gotten this bad. She would see that her life's direction was a mix of chances and choices, just like everyone else. Her own pattern of choices reinforced the life she currently was living. If she could maintain a high level of integrity she could keep her relationships strong, options open, and conflicts to a minimum, even during hard times. Alice could take stock of her daily actions to see where she might improve on her integrity.

Unfortunately, it's not easy to go from a life of low integrity to high integrity. A few big changes need to be made for that to happen. To uphold a high degree of integrity, you must first notice when you slip out of integrity. Alice, believed that she was upholding her integrity each day to the highest standard. With that perspective, there's no chance for a solution since she can't see a potential for improvement. Alice could prevent further damage to her relationships and financial status by noticing when she is not in integrity.

There are a few obstacles for Alice. From her perspective, the world is a difficult and unfair place. She was wrongfully arrested, her finances fell apart due to many events outside of her control, and her relationships are dissolving for reasons she can't understand. Think about this from Alice's point of view. Life looks bleak. It looks uncontrollable. She's disappointed, angry, sad, and scared. She's in reaction pretty much all the time.

Alice sees herself as a good girl. From her perspective, she is someone who always does the right thing and works hard. Alice's good girl identity is reflected in the way she talks. She speaks sweetly and rushes to be helpful to anyone in need. Since she sees herself as a good girl, everything that happens in her life is happening to a good girl who plays by the rules and works hard. When bad things happen to her, a good person who does everything right, then she assumes that she just can't win no matter how hard she tries. She can't see past her identity belief to see that she doesn't always behave like the good girl she pretends to be. This disconnect between how she sees herself and how she actually behaves is the root of her lack of integrity. There is a conflict between what she thinks she does and what she actually does.

Financially, Alice has convinced herself that she is not capable of making a larger salary than she has made in the past. In polite conversation where bolstering beliefs tend to be rampant, she says that she would like to go back to school so she could have a better career. More school would be too expensive and this bolstering belief tends to end the conversation about career change before it gets started. Alice lives on a tiny salary, but she's not close to making ends meet. She abuses any credit line that is extended her way. She does not stick to a budget or find ways to save money for emergencies. All of her money disappears days after she earns it. She's aware that her finances are a problem, and she believes that the solution is to make more money, which seems to her like it's impossible to do.

Alice has real problems. She has real debt, poor credit, and a perpetually empty bank account. She also has to rely on family to give her housing when she can't pay rent. Further, she is exhausting the generosity of her family and friends after many years of living like this. She's in real trouble. Not only that, but she goes into reaction each time she tries to face her problems. Alice's reaction shows itself in two ways. She switches into angry denial where she talks about how the world is unfair and she's having terrible luck or she goes into sweet denial where she talks about how everything is fine and she's got it all under control. What can she do to get past the denial phase?

Unfortunately, Alice is stuck right where she is until she can see her life from a different perspective. Her denial has gone on for many years and it could possibly go on for many more. You may be worried about getting stuck like Alice. To avoid getting stuck in this way, you can remember to ask yourself two questions each time you have a conflict. Question 1: In what ways am I out of integrity? Question 2: What have I been denying? Life is so complex that nearly everyone is in denial and out of integrity in some way all the time. If you have trouble finding the answers to these questions, then you are hiding something from yourself.

---

### Exercise: Denial

Denial is a wicked force. The answer can be right in your face, and you can't see it, but everyone else can.

To begin: Go to a trusted friend to ask their advice about something that has been bothering you. Ask them to tell you what you've been doing wrong. Don't speak. Don't agree or disagree with them. Just listen. Let them talk as long as they have something to share. Other people can see things about you that you are unable to see.

Why it works: The antidote to denial is to listen to what those around you have to say about you, especially when it triggers an emotional response.

Pitfalls: The statements that you want to deny or defend yourself against are the statements that touch you in a way that you haven't accepted yet. Feel the desire to defend and deny. Notice which things bring that feeling up in you. Use those feeling as a guide to find a new perspective.

---

If, like Alice, you go into reaction when you face your problems, try doing some ACC calibration. You can raise your emotional pain threshold so that your brain doesn't start screaming *Do something!* Instead of doing something, you can start to notice what's going on with your sensations and emotions. Until you can get your brain to stop screaming *Do something!*, you just run around like a chicken with your head cut off. The things you do under reactionary *Do something!* conditions are not productive in solving your problems.

Denial and going into reaction are both common ways to get stuck, but those aren't the only ways people get stuck. Alice's own identity compounded the problem of denial and further prevented her from shifting her perspective. Alice's belief that she is the proverbial good girl kept her from seeing that she might have had a hand in getting her life to this point. She maintains a facade of innocence for the world to see. She has a story of innocence that goes with her arrest and another story of innocence that goes with her financial troubles and a third story to go with her dissolving relationships. She spends a lot of time talking about how much she is doing right in her life.

People who get through conflict gracefully spend a little time in denial too, but they eventually grasp a new perspective and move on through the steps of letting go of their belief. The conversion from denial to perspective shift is something you can sense when you watch it happen to someone.[20] A person in denial is disgusted, holds an upright stiff body position, and acts a little put off. A person who has grasped that they have a responsibility in the problem has a more relaxed, fallen, and humble look. The difference is distinct.

You can feel the difference in your own body through sensation and emotion when you discover your responsibility in your conflict. Are you stiff and put off? Are you fallen and humble? The change doesn't just happen in your body. Your thoughts change too. In denial you are thinking about all the outside forces that are negatively affecting your life. In perspective shift you start to have the reluctant acceptance that you have been your own worst enemy. You will still actively defend your choices and actions in the perspective shift stage, but once you can see things from a new perspective, you are on your way to letting go of your key belief.

Alice still hasn't learned her key belief. She's stuck arguing that the bolstering beliefs are her real problems. She argues that her life would be very different if she had more money, but it's probably obvious to you by now that money is not her real problem. Her financial struggles are a symptom of living with a lack of integrity for a long time. To find her key belief, Alice would have to shift her perspective to see how she has a responsibility in her own life's patterns.

---

[20] To see how someone's face and posture changes when perspective shift happens, watch "I Am Not Your Guru" the Tony Robbins documentary which is available on Netflix.

Alice got stuck in the denial phase. She can't see how many of her problems are within her control. It's as though Alice thinks that other people are building the walls in her fortress. It's very common for people to have trouble making that initial perspective shift. Once you are able to see your situation from various perspectives, you will be free of the shackles of the denial phase, but there's more work to be done. Even after you see a path to improving your life, it's possible you may get stuck while navigating that path.

---

## Exercise - Getting out of Reaction

When you are trying to have a meaningful conversation, but you find yourself in reaction, you aren't able to listen or think very well.

To begin: The next time you find yourself in reaction. Notice your internal state. Say to yourself or out loud, "I feel angry, confused, and frustrated." Or whatever set of emotions are going on inside you. Take your time. Let your internal climate settle before you open your mouth to say anything other than your own emotions.

Be careful about responding directly to the other person at first. They will ask questions like, "Why are you angry?" Don't answer them. If you do, you'll be giving your emotions over to reasons which is a recipe for staying in reaction. Feel the way your body feels. Listen to the thoughts swirl in your head. Make a decision not to say very much and to only speak the truth.

Why it works: Noticing your feelings in the moment allows you to connect with truth. Instead of attaching your feelings to your thoughts, you let thoughts and feelings stay independent of each other. Telling the other person how you feel allows them to notice you instead of getting stuck in their own experience.

Pitfalls: If you are intensely angry during a conversation and you use this process to stay out of reaction, you might not have much to say. When you choose to speak only the truth, but your mind is clouded by emotion, you won't have many true thoughts beyond voicing your emotions. That's ok. The other person will get the idea.

---

# Paul's Story: The Unspeakable Block

When you get stuck *after* the perspective shift phase, it's as though you can see yourself building walls and reinforcing them, but you can't seem to stop. You can't start to dismantle the wall or find the key belief. Paul's story is about getting stuck, not at denial, but in the feeling phase. You must follow your feelings to find the key belief.

Paul was a recent college graduate who was struggling to find his place in the world. He'd been a good student and he got a job right out of school, but he wasn't happy. He wanted to start his own company. He'd been working on the idea for a few years already, but hadn't made much progress. He was torn between looking for a meaningful job or working on his startup in earnest. His bank account was dwindling and he was starting to feel a lot of stress.

He complained that employers didn't see his true self when he was applying for jobs. He also said that he found himself working on his startup whenever he had downtime. It was a bit of an obsession.

Although his bank account was low, he wanted to forget about looking for a job and instead he just wanted to build the company. The company he wanted to build was particularly challenging and would require a lot of resources. He needed to connect with strategic partners or find something he could leverage to get started. That launching point never seemed to materialize. Yet, he was obsessed with the idea. It was distracting him in his daily life. When Paul talked about his startup, he had an energy behind his words. He seemed angry.

The problem was that when Paul didn't have anything productive to do, he turned to focus on his startup. Paul's frustrations were mounting. He wanted to start the company so that he could save people from financial predators. Paul's idea was to build a fair lending company for those with bad credit. There was nothing wrong with his idea, but his timing was off. He didn't have a good business argument for starting this company with no resources. He did have a fire lit behind his sense of motivation.

Ideally, Paul could put the startup idea away until he gathered the proper resources to get it off the ground. He would be able to focus on making a bit of money first. He would identify the skills, partners, and resources that he would need to get started. Then, when the time was right, he could launch in earnest. But his obsession continued and he kept putting time into the startup instead of finding a job.

Paul used MindSET to get to the bottom of his problem. He started by venting his frustrations. He documented himself complaining about how employers didn't know the real Paul so getting a job wasn't going well. He also heard himself say repeatedly that he was angry about injustice and that's why he wanted to start his company. He said a lot of other things too, but those were the two notions that he said with the most energy. He was emotionally heated when he spoke of injustice and he was visibly dejected when he spoke of employers not being able to know the real him. Paul knew that he needed to spend some time with those two notions "The real Paul" and "Injustice." Clearly there was something important for him in those two thoughts.

Paul knew that he needed to shift his perspective. He had to stop seeing "injustice" in the context of his startup and he had to stop seeing "The real Paul" in terms of employers. He looked at a more fundamental context for those two notions. What might "The real Paul" mean to him? Who didn't know the real Paul? What injustice might he have endured?

Paul thought about whether he had suffered injustice in his own life. Remember, at the beginning, every conflict looks like it's not about you, and yet every conflict is about you. When you find yourself worried about other people, check to see what you are worried about with yourself. At some point Paul felt injustice and instead of simply noticing it, he attached that feeling to the poor and underserved. It became a belief that started to fuel his motivation to save people. Every time Paul felt injustice, he wanted to work on his company. But what was the injustice in his life? He still didn't know.

MindSET works because it uses all three channels of information. Sensation and emotion connect you with truth (but it is a meaningless truth). When you are connected to truth (by feeling), you have a better chance at recognizing and disposing of false thoughts. Paul couldn't just think about the ideas *injustice* and *the real Paul*. Thinking alone would surely lead him to false answers. He had to follow the feelings that came with those notions. All he knew was that he felt anger. Paul was familiar with MindSET. He knew that he needed to use his sense of emotion to help him find his belief. He got the most angry when he talked about his startup and so that became a good starting point for his search for a key belief. It might seem funny that he wanted to work on a company that caused him to feel angry, but it makes sense. He had buried his conflict in that company idea. His brain wouldn't let him forget about it. The company didn't make him angry, the conflict did.

Paul thought back to his childhood and early adolescence. Many conflicts stem from early years when we learn the rules of the world. Those rules become beliefs and many years later pop up as conflicts. When Paul went into his memories to find an injustice he suffered, he remembered that he was bullied in school. He was looking for a memory that had a feeling attached to it. To use MindSET, you follow the feelings, not the thoughts. Unfortunately, his memory of injustice didn't have any feelings associated with it. In fact, when he thought about the past, his feelings all seemed to disappear.

Since MindSET uses thoughts and feelings together to uncover beliefs, it can be hard to proceed when all feelings seem to shut down. Feelings are an anchor to truth. Without a connection to feelings, you can't be sure that your thoughts aren't just playing tricks on you. Paul was stuck.

When a person has ignored feelings for a long time, the feelings can be hard to revive. A memory that seems to have no feelings attached to it at all, might actually have a lot of associated feelings that have been carefully turned into beliefs. Paul admitted that, in general, he felt anger and not much else. He was having trouble feeling the rest of his emotions. Joy, disgust, sadness, and fear were simply not available for him. He knew he needed those feelings to get to the bottom of his conflict. How do you revive unavailable feelings?

Often feelings are held back along with some thoughts that have been held back. If you are having trouble feeling all of your emotions, ask yourself if there is something you've been keeping back. Is there anything you've neglected to say out loud. Is there anything you've been hiding from someone? Paul had been keeping back a big piece of information from people very important to him. Paul hadn't told his family that he's gay. He tried to tell himself that it wasn't a big deal. He rationalized that it wasn't his parents' business who he wanted to have relationships with.

The truth was that he did want them to know. He wanted his parents to know the real Paul and the effort that it took to hide that piece of himself from his parents was also hiding his emotions from himself.

Paul knew he needed to break the silence with his parents. He made a plan to invite them to visit. He would share his news, which would end the long-standing block in honest communication. He didn't know what he would feel, but he was willing to feel whatever emotions came. He was prepared to notice if he went into reaction. If he found himself in reaction, he knew what to do. He would notice his current emotions and sensations which would automatically bring him back to presence and truth. He was careful to avoid pretending that he knew where his emotions were coming from. He was prepared to simply feel them.

You may wonder what it's like to use MindSET with your family when they are completely unfamiliar with MindSET. There's an interesting thing that happens when one person in a group is able to be present. Even though the rest of the people in the group are not trained in how to be present, or how to deal with conflict, they act as though they are somewhat familiar with this training. It's like putting a drop of blue dye in a glass of water. The dye is concentrated at first, but tends to spread throughout the whole glass eventually. Presence is the same way. When one person is present, the other people in the room tend to wake up and become more present too. Paul was able to talk to his family with presence and authenticity and they were able to talk to him in the same way. Presence is like emotion in that it can be transmitted through empathy too.

Paul's family did have some strong emotions when they heard his news. He was willing to experience their feelings and see them work through whatever had to come. He didn't judge their feelings. He didn't know where their feelings came from any more than he knew where his feelings came from. He wasn't tempted to equate their feelings with support, love, caring, acceptance, or lack thereof. He knew their emotions were unrelated to those things.

Before Paul broke his silence, he described himself as cynical and he said he had a chip on his shoulder. He was angry much of the time. His anger was affecting his ability to find his place in the world. Whenever he considered getting a better paying job or taking on a new consulting client, he found himself more angry and backed off from pursuing the opportunity further. Paul had stopped feeling emotions other than anger. As he got emotionally constipated, the anger increased. He didn't realize at first that keeping a secret from his family was affecting him as much as it did. He'd decided that his sexual preference was no big deal and he didn't need to tell them. Fortunately, he realized that hiding things from his family was causing him trouble.

When it comes to sharing our own secrets, we tend to fear backlash, or anger, or some scary unknown. We think that the world won't accept us if it knew the truth of how horrible we are inside. The reality is that we all have something or many things that we think are unspeakable. When we fail to share those things with loved ones, we limit the closeness of those relationships. Intimacy is impossible when there are secrets. When we have secrets, we think that the other person will not be able to love us as much if they knew the truth. In fact, love is blocked by the existence of the secret. Exposing the secret allows love and emotion to flow again.

Paul's secret was blocking him from feeling any emotions beyond anger. He was starting to feel like no one was able to see the real version of him. He was obsessed with injustice. All of these things lifted off of him when he shared his secret with his parents. Just a week later, he was able to express and feel joy. He said he was able to cry and he started to feel emotions from others through empathy. He was excited for the future and was starting to think positively about what he might do for work next. He looked like a different person. His face was brighter and his movements seemed effortless.

Paul's key belief was that he needed to hide his sexuality. He didn't realize all of the other implications in making the choice to hide. He didn't see how it was impossible to have a healthy romantic relationship while he was still unwilling to talk to his parents about his true feelings. He wasn't able to process his emotions while he was hiding a big secret from people who were fundamental in his life. He also didn't understand how his own interests and desire to be productive at work was wrapped up in hiding himself. He got so good at hiding himself that he was hiding himself from everything in his life. By letting go of that key belief, he was able to participate fully in life.

After Paul made the decision to stop hiding, he was able to feel more than just anger. As his anger subsided, he was able to feel his more nuanced emotions. He thought back to his childhood and his experience of being bullied. Those memories felt different to him. He saw that he wasn't actually bullied, but instead he didn't feel accepted in school. That feeling of not fitting in extended beyond his school and into his hometown. He felt stuck there, cornered in a situation where he had no other options. At once he understood his obsession with starting a lending company for people who had bad credit and no other options. He wasn't obsessed with finance, he was obsessed with creating options for people, like himself, who were cornered in situations where they'd run out of options.

With a new understanding of his own motivations, Paul was able to make a conscious decision about whether he would put time into a lending company or spend his time in other ways. He could follow his appetite instead of following his compulsion. Also, he no longer had the emotional block that was preventing him from feeling his nuanced emotions. This newfound channel of information allowed him to communicate with others in a way that was much deeper than before.

After Paul came out to his parents about his sexual orientation, he wondered if he needed to learn how to be gay. He figured he had to change his identity so that he could fully embrace who he truly is. Identity is a tricky thing. We feel like we need to know who we are. We cling to titles like Artist, Businessperson, Gay, Straight, Catholic, and Jewish, but those labels never seem to fully describe all of the aspects of ourselves. When Paul thought he needed to adopt a new gay self, I reminded him that identity isn't real. It's an illusion. I encouraged Paul to connect with the selfless self. Here's what I mean by that.

Each one of us has a kernel of self deep down that has no history, no future, no name, no sexual preference, no finances, no parents, no children, no education, no nothing. That self is the difference between a human body containing life and a lifeless body. That unfettered life is the true self. When Paul felt compelled to adopt a new identity, instead he connected to that true self and he found that it calmed his need to label himself. He understood that he could behave in whatever way felt natural, he could date whoever felt natural to date, and he could be productive in whatever way suited his appetite.

# Roger's Story: The Power of Identity

Identity is an illusion that limits people from their full potential. Alice's identity being the good girl prevented her from seeing the truth of her actions. Identity can fool you into thinking that you are not capable of certain aptitudes like Melissa discovered when she switched her major to computer science. The next story is from Roger. He struggled with reading in school. You might think that sounds like the farthest thing away from an identity issue, but you'd be missing something.

Roger is in college and is struggling. He is actively social and has no trouble making friends, but he feels like he's not smart. He feels less capable than the other people in his classes. Roger takes hours to get through his homework. He reads the same sentence over and over and can't make progress through his work. When Roger tries to do his schoolwork, instead of learning, Roger goes into reaction. He gets angry, shouts, and rages. Sometimes he throws things.

Roger is ready to get through this problem. He is thinking about what he'd like to do for work when school is over. He knows that he's not going to be able to get a good job if he goes into reaction whenever he comes up against something challenging for him. Ideally, Roger would be able to see his limitations and push against them in ways that didn't cause him to become angry. Everyone has limitations, but when your limitations cause you to go into reaction, it's a double whammy. You can't listen or learn when you are in reaction. Pushing past limitations requires presence.

Reading wasn't the only thing in Roger's life that he felt angry about. He was also haunted by the feeling that he had been abandoned by his mother. You see, Roger had been adopted by a white American family who found him in an orphanage in rural Asia. He was three when he was adopted and he had a few memories from his early days. He had struggled all of his life with anger and rage.

Roger is involved in a community of people who use sensation and emotion to allow them to distinguish between true and false logic. They don't call their method MindSET but it is the same process as MindSET. The process has been used by people for many hundreds of years and it has arisen multiple times under various names. You might expect that it's likely that multiple people would independently discover how to use their bodies to experience the world with expert clarity. Roger was familiar with an equivalent to the MindSET process, but he was still stuck feeling angry about being abandoned and angry about his limitations in the classroom.

Roger followed his anger. He followed his feelings of abandonment and his feelings of academic inadequacy and worked to find a shift in his perspective. Roger spent time in a group setting talking about his feelings and how they were affecting his life. Group settings can be very helpful because others can often see what's going on with you even when you can't see it yourself. Another person in the group made a comment at just the right time when Roger was open to hearing it. She asked him whether he was willing to give up the orphanage so that he could excel in his life. To me, and probably to you, that comment doesn't make much sense. The comment might have just flown by unheard if Roger weren't prepared to accept it. To Roger, the comment made all the sense in the world and it hit him like an arrow through the heart. It was exactly the perspective he needed to hear.

Roger realized that he didn't feel abandoned by his mother. Not exactly. He felt afraid that he was the one who abandoned her. He now lived in a comfortable developed world with money and food and an education. His biological family was still in rural Asia suffering the challenges of poverty. Roger was afraid that he would further abandon his Asian family if he were to embrace all that his American life could offer. He connected this conflict to his education. Each time he had to break through a new educational challenge, the conflict put him into reaction.

Did you catch the key belief that was holding up the wall in Roger's fortress? He didn't say it outright, but you might be able to glean what it was. Roger believed that if he were to embrace all that his American life had to offer, that he would automatically have to abandon his Asian family. This is an identity belief. Identity often feels like it connects us to our families or heritage. It feels like we might disrespect our people if we behave differently from the way they behave.

Compare Roger's identity belief with Paul's problem. Are there any similarities? Might Paul have worried that his family would abandon him if he told them the truth about his romantic preferences? Might he have worried that he had to abandon his values and family ideals so that he could stop *living a lie*. Roger worried about abandonment too. His relationship with his Asian family was very distant in the sense that he didn't know them or communicate with them, but it was very close in the sense that he longed to be a part of that family in spite of the distance. He didn't want anything to make that distance seem larger.

Identity is a powerful illusion. We attach our sense of belonging and acceptance to our identities, but it doesn't have to be that way. You can have comfort and belonging without using identity to get there. You can recognize that benefit permanence works with identity too. Just like the benefit that you get when you think about your teddy bear that you haven't seen in years, you can feel a kinship with a community even though you no longer subscribe to the beliefs and behaviors of that community anymore. You can have the emotional benefits of having once had an identity without holding on tightly to it. Identity is comforting, reassuring, and helpful in many cases, but it also acts as a barrier to change.

A fluid identity is one that changes with your interests and activities. Alternatively, you can have a minimal identity that labels very little of who you are. Some people are able to abandon the illusion of identity altogether. You get to decide how much you subscribe to your illusion of identity. When you have little to no identity, you are able to connect with people based on empathy and compassion, instead of shared activities, similar upbringing, shared beliefs, or the other elements that we usually use to find common ground. It's very freeing to live with a small or flexible identity. You have fewer conflicts and more options.

Roger began to see that his identity as an orphaned child was limiting his ability to take advantage of the opportunities around him. A person with a strong identity will judge opportunities; they are either *for a person like me* or *not for a person like me*. Scholastic success was an opportunity that Roger judged, *not for a person like me*. Now, after uncovering this key belief, Roger sees how he can increase his connection to his Asian family by making money and regularly visiting the village of his birth as he did once as a teenager. He could study his native language or meet others who were also adopted from the same part of the world. A good education won't hurt his chances of connecting with his people.

Identity was an underlying belief that created conflicts for many of the people in these stories. Identity can be both a bolstering belief and a key belief. You may start and end your hero's journey thinking about your identity. Alice's good girl persona convinced her that she could do no wrong. Paul was afraid he had to become someone new just because he stopped being secretive about his sexuality. Roger had a bolstering belief that he wasn't one of the smart people in school, and that let him to a realization that he had been identifying himself as an orphan all these years. Think back to the other stories in this book. Can you find the identity beliefs in their stories? Melissa didn't see herself as worthy member of the coder community at first. The Russians played roles acting like berating wife and angry husband. Val believed that he had to save the world like Batman. What identities do you have?

## Author's Story: The Little Things

Relationships are fundamental to the human experience. No matter who you are, you care, on some level, what other people think of you. You can be a fiercely independent person and still, you cannot help but entertain thoughts about your relationships with others on occasion. There's no way around it. The human brain is social. It's perpetually open to inputs from others.

Developing your ability to communicate and connect with others can feel like a big hurdle. Where do you start? How do you improve your relationships in your professional life and personal life? Your relationships, no matter what kind of relationship, are shaped by your beliefs and conflicts in ways that are very specific to you. You can improve all of your relationships in one fell swoop when you find and retire a belief that has been limiting your ability to communicate with others. I know this to be true from my own experience.

When I retired a key belief, I improved my professional and personal relationships dramatically. Although my life didn't seem to be drastically limited (I was enjoying success in many areas of my life) I felt like there was a better way to interact with others. I was a strongly independent person who preferred to work alone and spend my downtime alone. I enjoyed being social, but it took a lot of energy out of me to be with others. It felt like I had to put up with other's needs and desires and there wasn't room for my own needs and desires. I realized that I was going to have to make a change in the way I dealt with others so that I could grow in business and in my personal life.

I noticed a pattern lurking in my life. I did not ask for what I wanted. In fact, I did everything in my power to hide what I wanted from others. When I was alone, I could indulge in what I wanted, so being alone was preferable to being with other people. This pattern affected the little things and the big things. If I wanted pizza for dinner, I was sure to hide that information from anyone around me. I went into reaction and froze up when it came time to express my desire for something as simple as pizza. I behaved the same in the case of big things too. If I wanted to talk about something with my partner or ask for something at work, I avoided the topic. I would convince myself that I had broached conversations and that my desires were shot down. Now, I look back and see that I avoided those conversations and pretended otherwise.

What do you do with the knowledge that you tend to avoid asking for what you want? When you know this about yourself, how can you stop the self-destructive behavior? I didn't know the answer to that question for a long time. All I could do was watch myself create barriers by not sharing my desires with those around me.

I learned how to follow my feelings to find beliefs. I followed my own irritation, sadness, and a coldness toward others and found that I believed I wasn't allowed to want. I was able to clearly defend this belief. My parents had taught me that you don't get what you want in life. They taught me to hide what pleases you so that no one takes it away. The lesson wasn't explicitly relayed to me this way. Instead, I learned this lesson over and over through daily interactions. Each holiday I was generously given gifts, but rarely the one item that I had expressly wanted. Over the years, I grew to believe that my parents, who are wonderful and generous people, were teaching me a very important lesson in life - hide what you want, so that you have some chance of getting it. I trusted this lesson implicitly.

I knew my behavior was a barrier to my development in my business and personal life and I knew where the behavior came from, but I was still unable to let it go. I was still compelled to hide what I wanted even when I knew it was hurting me. Without thinking too hard about it, I stayed with that notion for weeks. *I can't openly want things.* How can I learn to want things? What might my life be like if I can want things?

For weeks, I felt intense emotions that seemed not to be attached to wanting, but maybe they were, who knows? I felt anger one day, sadness another day. I felt bitterness that seemed like it had something to do with my family another day. The day I got to the bottom of my belief, I was feeling short-tempered. I was mountain biking with friends and I didn't feel like spending time with them. I sent them ahead and fought up the mountain on my own. Grumpy and irritated, I felt like indulging myself and not wasting energy on other people. As I struggled through the effort of pedaling my bike up steep inclines and over rocks, the fight and effort in my body was a mix of athleticism and sheer rage. I was pretty sure that if I stopped biking and sat down for a while I would continue to breathe hard and sweat as part of a temper tantrum instead of exercise. In the midst of my own emotional hiss and spittle, I realized why my belief was not true. I crashed my bike about a minute later.

I had believed that my parents had taught me the valuable lesson of not wanting. They did this by carefully avoiding any specific gifts or other requests that I made. We had enough money for these gifts; I wasn't asking for anything extravagant. For decades I thought this was a lesson that was meant to fortify me against an unjust and accommodating world. When I specifically asked for something, I was given something different, often similar to my request, but not what I had asked for. Even simple requests for inexpensive items were disregarded and instead I was given something else. I was perplexed by my parents' behavior. I tried to make sense of the disappointment each time. Instead of noticing my feelings, I shuttled them into reasons and beliefs. Eventually, those beliefs developed into the one I was hunting, *I can't openly want.*

As I connected with the physicality of my exercise-induced rage, I connected with truth. A thought arose. My parents weren't teaching me a lesson about wanting. My parents were simply not listening to me. When I asked for a specific brand of jeans, they heard that I needed pants and bought me three pairs of some other random kind of pants. When I asked for a baseball glove, I was given rollerblades. When I wanted camping equipment, I got a jacket. Like most people, my parents were listening to me through their own filters of belief and conflict. My life lesson of not wanting wasn't a life lesson at all. It was a side effect of a human foible. My parents were terrible listeners. I was stunned and inconsolable when I discovered where my belief came from.

I cried as though I were witnessing a funeral. It felt like I was mourning the death of a young person. I couldn't tell if my body ached with sadness or ached because I had injured myself in the bike crash. It was both. I ached all over. While I cried, I had no distinct thoughts beyond, "This feels terrible and I can't wait until it's over." I was emotionally wiped out for a few days afterward. I felt like a wet washrag - unaffected and limp.

That realization, that I had mistaken my parent's quirks for a fundamental life lesson, was pivotal in allowing me to drop my belief post haste. I knew my life could be different from then on. However, I had never learned how to want in a healthy way. I never learned how to have conversations with others about what I wanted. I shared my revelations with close friends in hopes that they might overlook any awkward attempts to discuss my desires or preferences. I asked them to be patient with me if I was shy about making requests.

From the outside, it looked like nothing changed for me. I didn't run out and buy a bunch of things. I didn't change anything material about the way I was living. However, the way I thought about things changed immensely. I was able to make restaurant suggestions and veto the places I didn't want to eat. I was able to relax in a social setting for multiple days without having to take alone-time breaks. I was able to negotiate some business arrangements and the negotiation felt like beautiful teamwork instead of an exhausting scrimmage. Instead of going into reaction when I wanted something, I was able to tell people that I wanted something. I didn't always get what I wanted, but that was ok; just being able to want openly was like an emancipation.

In some ways, my belief was a little thing. It didn't stop me from wanting and it didn't stop me from pursuing the things I wanted. Instead, it controlled the way I interacted with other people when I wanted something. I saw other people as though they were in the way of the things I wanted because I couldn't communicate my desires. No one was in my way. I maintained and defended that wall in my belief fortress all by myself. I defended the barrier. No one else was capable of helping me get around it either. How could they? The moment I wanted something, I hid it from everyone who might help me achieve it.

I picture my belief fortress to have rubble where that wall used to be. It's still something I have to navigate. If I were walking in my fortress, I would have to climb over bits of rock and mortar. In life, I have to purposefully make decisions to share my desires with others. I have to overcome a small barrier that feels like a momentary hesitation. I have caught myself thinking old thoughts like, "I'll just go be alone so I don't have to put up with other people's desires." When those old thoughts arise, I'm not a slave to them anymore. I can choose a different tack. I can remember to speak up and share what I want in a way that feels authentic to my true feelings and compassionate of those around me.

Retiring my belief allows me to have authentic conversations with people about what I want without going into reaction about it. I can now advocate for my own desires without having to resort to anger or frustration. If things don't go my way in the end, it's ok because my desires were heard and taken into consideration. My belief came from a misunderstanding and I had a hard time letting go of it. Even when I could see it was hurting me, I held on tight.

Imagine how many ways I might have gotten stuck looking for that belief. If I got stuck like Alice, I would have defended my behavior and insisted that I was right in hiding my desires. Or I might not have noticed my pattern of hiding desires at all. I could have gotten stuck like Paul if I had trouble feeling the emotions surrounding that belief. Physical activity was instrumental in helping me find insight. I might not have been able to connect to my sensations and emotions if I weren't out doing something physically active. I could have focused too much on the logic behind my belief and lost myself in the philosophy of desire and what it means to want. I could have focused my attention on blaming my parents for teaching me a lesson that didn't serve me well. Finally, I might not have been willing to follow through with purposefully sharing my desires with other people. Even after I let go of my belief, I still had to close the circle. Every day, I have to hold up my own integrity and be conscious of communicating my needs and wants without creating the expectation that I will always get what I want.

## Summary of Key Concepts

- Life is different after you find your key beliefs and retire them. You will feel less stressed, and less busy since your mind isn't constantly chewing on conflict.

- Each belief has a life of it's own. You can't just go through this process once and eradicate your beliefs.

- The beliefs you initially discover will be bolstering beliefs.

- Once you are able to see your situation from various perspectives, you will be free of the shackles of the denial phase, but there's more work to be done

- To use MindSET, you need to follow the feelings, not the thoughts. Let both true and false thoughts come freely while you focus on the feelings.

- If you are having trouble feeling all of your emotions, ask yourself if there is something you've been keeping back. Is there anything that has gone unsaid?

- Group settings can be very helpful because others can often see what's going on with you even when you can't see it yourself.

- As always, follow the emotion to the belief. Physical activity can help open your sensation and emotion channels.

# 8: New Manners

*Practice not-doing, and everything will fall into place.*

Tao Te Ching, Stephen Mitchell's version

Much of this book has focused on noticing as the way to overcome many of the challenges you have with conflict, emotion, and beliefs. Noticing might seem like an impotent suggestion at first. It is an undeniably simple thing to do and the simplicity of the noticing leads many people to disregard its value as a solution. How can the simple act of noticing possibly solve serious problems in your life that you've carried with you for a long time?

You know the answer to that question now. The ACC, the *Do something!* part of your brain, responds to calibration. Noticing is the action that turns the calibration knob. When you start to regularly notice without acting, within only a few weeks you become less irritable, less reactionary, and less compelled to behave in ways that you may come to regret. Keep up with your noticing and you could live the rest of your life in a more level-headed way. Conflict isn't solved through noticing alone, but make noticing a regular part of your life and you will be better equipped to end your conflicts.

I was taught to notice on my first day in a group setting as part of the MindSET-type training I learned under Judith Orloff M.Ed. My training lasted about five months, but I was able to start noticing on day one. I was surprised to discover that I had not been noticing the world, I had been observing it. The difference between observing and noticing is as spectacular as the difference between a black and white photo and color television. Observing was a cold and distant act that I could do while remaining removed from the thing or person observed. Noticing is something I realized I needed my whole self, my whole MindSET to do. Noticing includes feeling whereas observing can be done with logic only. Ask yourself, am I noticing, or am I just observing?

If you get nothing more from this book beyond the benefits of noticing your ease in life will still improve dramatically. Noticing is the basis of meditation just like noticing is the basis of ACC calibration. It's the magic behind the mysticism of Buddhism. Compare for a moment two people: one who never learns to calibrate her ACC and the other who is very skilled at ACC calibration. The one who has gained powerful control over her own reactions to emotion, to physical pain, and to uncertainty may seem like she has magical powers to the person who is a slave to her increasingly reactive, uncalibrated ACC. You too can have those magical powers. They aren't magical at all. The things you can do with a calibrated ACC seem unbelievable when you've lived without a way of controlling your reactions. The ACC comes standard with the human body, you just have to calibrate it.

Once you dial your *Do something!* threshold up to a level where you can begin to listen, the magic really starts. Getting out of reaction is like taking the cotton out of your ears. You can stop shouting and start hearing everything clearly. You will hear that the answers have been right in front of you the whole time. You can easily distinguish between truth and fiction. You can hear what people are really telling you, not just the polite surface banter. Your decisions become obvious and clear. Illusions are still present, but you know they are illusions. How can you start parsing truth from fiction, knowing what's real, and seeing illusions when those powers have been the stuff of magic until now?

When I was four, I sat cross-legged in front of the television. The friendly character, Mr. Rogers, asked me a question and I answered him. My mother heard me talking to the television and told me that Mr. Rogers couldn't hear me because the image on the screen is a picture of him, not really him. I remember being embarrassed and a little bit ashamed that I didn't know that the people on television couldn't hear me. It took a moment of clarity to shift my world. I thought, "Yeah, Mr. Rogers is pretty small and flat and he disappears when I push this button so I guess it makes sense that he isn't really here." My ego was bruised for a moment, but I never went back to thinking the people in the TV could hear me. The shift you are making now is the same kind of shift. Your ego will be bruised for a moment and then you will never go back to being confused again.

The world is mostly made of fiction. We talk about the polite surface problems that don't have anything to do with our real challenges deep inside. Identity is a mask that we've grown so used to wearing that we forget we can take it off. Even our fundamental motivations for going to work, starting families, and getting out of bed in the morning are based on beliefs that are only as true as we will them to be. We create mental rulebooks that define which parts of the world are available to us and which parts are separate from us. This is all fiction and there is nothing wrong with fiction. It's the way humans do life.

However, you likely have never seen the fiction of the world as clearly as you may be able to see it now. And what is fiction if not simply an acceptable form of lie? You may feel embarrassed and a little bit ashamed that you didn't see through the fiction all this time. You may feel more intense emotions about it too. That's ok. The world has always been full of lies and will continue to be full of lies. Nothing has changed except that you can now tell the difference between truth and lies. You may find yourself longing for truth. Until recently, you were used to believing that the world was full of truth and that lies were rare and harmful. Just like I was able to get over the fact that Mr. Rogers wasn't really in my living room, you will get over this shift too. It will take a bit of adjustment, but you will be comfortable in the world again shortly.

Truth is rare. It happens only occasionally and it will begin to stand out to you like fireworks. Those who still have the cotton of reaction in their ears can't hear truth any differently than fiction. It's too muffled. Those who have conflicts and who defend their beliefs like guards defend a fortress can't hear truth any differently than fiction. It's the person who has stopped defending, who has stopped pushing, and ceased living up to anything other than integrity who can hear truth clearly. When they hear it, what do they do? Nothing, because they are not compelled by conflict and reaction. Truth needs no defense, so there is nothing to do.

# Going Deeper

This chapter marks the end to this step in your guided learning. I encourage you to keep using noticing and MindSET long after you put the book down. The more beliefs you retire and the more you calibrate your ACC, the more at peace you will be in your life and in the world. You will be able to follow whatever appetite you discover for yourself. You will be able to handle extreme adversity and gut-wrenching change with grace. To achieve that sense of peace, you have to keep going. You have more fortress walls to crumble. It's unlikely that you have retired all of your conflict-causing beliefs. You could argue that you have no more problems, but you'd be in denial.

I encourage you to start your own MindSET group. A MindSET Group is an informal gathering of two or more people who have read this book and now understand how beliefs and conflict work. A MindSET Group is not much different from a book club; it's a place to discuss your experiences, understandings, and talk about how you might be stuck. Together, you have a greater chance of finding and retiring beliefs. Everyone in the group will come with different perspectives and this allows you to help each other to overcome the initial hurdles of perspective shift. You will have different beliefs and you'll find that different experiences put you into reaction.

When you can see someone else in reaction over an experience that doesn't register an emotion for you, it's much easier to understand how conflicts are not universal. Your reactions are connected to your individual beliefs. It can also be helpful to take a poll between two or more people to ask, "Do you believe this is true?" When a given belief isn't universally accepted, then you know it's fiction. If you start a MindSET Group, please feel free to reach out to me through www.mindsetyourmanners.com so I can add the group to a worldwide list of MindSET Groups.

Once you can see how much of the world is made of fiction, you may be desperate to share that news with others. When your friends and family have problems, you'll want to point out their bolstering beliefs and show them how they can get rid of their conflicts. Remember that misery loves company. Misery does not take kindly to advice. If you try to insist that your friend's money problems are not really about money, you may lose a friend. Beliefs seem as real as gravity to those who maintain them and if you try to force people to see that they've been misinterpreting their lives, they will view you as a jerk. Go ahead. Test the waters, but give up if they can't hear you. They are most likely in reaction anyway. Instead, give them a copy of this book. When they are ready and willing, they will read it, but no sooner.

Instead of talking about MindSET, live it. Listen with your sensations, emotions, and thoughts. Be as aware as you want to be. Notice. Do the exercises. Your view of the world will change and with it, you will wake up to more and more truth. Those who pay attention to you, your spouse, children, parents, colleagues, and friends will begin to wake up, too. Awareness transmits much like emotion, through empathy.

You will continue to grow and see things in a new light for a long time after reading this book. The ripple effect in your own life may take months. The additive effects of transmitting awareness to your friends and family could take years. I encourage you to keep learning about awareness and unlearning your beliefs.

# Fresh Eyes

If I've done my job as your guide, I've opened your eyes to the possibility of new perspectives and new insights. You may choose to immerse yourself deeply in uncovering beliefs or you may stop your efforts at doing three minutes of ACC exercises before bed. If you do nothing else, calibrating your ACC to a less reactive threshold will improve your ability to navigate the world.

Your depth of commitment to calibrating your ACC and retiring your beliefs will show in your results. You have the chance to experience some distinct changes in your life. The rest of this chapter serves to give you a bit of guidance as you use MindSET in your daily experience, particularly as you take the inward work you've been doing and begin to apply it outward to your relationships and interpersonal communications.

## Empathy

You have always had empathy, the ability to feel the emotions of others, but you may have never noticed it before. Or, even if you noticed it, you may have not known what to do with it. You may have felt emotions through empathy, decided they were yours, and responded by going into reaction. As you feel through your own backlog of emotions, your emotional net will clear and you will be more receptive to feeling the emotions of others. You may start to notice intense emotions that follow some people as though they have their own personal weather cloud. You can feel emotions and not hold onto them. Let them pass through your net. Don't collect emotions.

When I first became sensitive to empathy, I found myself in a very intense meeting at a university administrators office. This woman was acting very pleasant and accommodating to me. Would I like tea? How was my drive over? But I had the distinct feeling that she was screaming for help in a panic. I knew that she was screaming. Her calm exterior was the illusion and the screaming was the truth. I wasn't hallucinating. I could see her sitting calmly on the other side of the desk. My body felt as though I were in a room with a screaming person. I felt like screaming too. I felt like bolting from the room as though it were on fire. I managed to use noticing exercises to get through the *Do something!* experience of being in reaction and get to a place where I could talk to her. We chatted for a while and the conversation seemed contentious. Was it me? Was it her? What was going on?

I noticed my desire to flee. I noticed the heat in my face and the fight in my chest. Then, I was able to get out of reaction and really listen to her. She revealed that she had been reprimanded recently, presumably by a dean. I was talking to her about my ideas on career development for her students, and she wasn't allowed to execute on those ideas. By meeting with me, she was disobeying her boss's wishes and wasting my time. She was doing so because she thought her students needed career development support, but she wasn't allowed to do anything about it. When I discovered that truth, the screaming made a lot of sense. I thanked her for her time and went on my way with my eyes open a little wider.

You may discover that being around a specific person inspires you to feel intense emotions. You are likely experiencing empathy. Use MindSET to stay out of reaction so that you can listen and be compassionate toward others. Some people who are new to feeling empathy find that they have a short period of time, days or weeks, when they just can't deal with how intense other people's emotions feel to them. This phase will pass. It's temporary.

## Seeing lies

You will not only feel other people's emotions, you will see through their lies and bolstering beliefs. This ability to see fiction is particularly challenging at first. When people lie to you, they have no intention of coming clean. They may not even know they are lying. They may be lying to themselves too. So, there's not much value in telling them that you know they are lying. The world is full of lies anyway. Instead of judging lies as bad or wrong, you can hear the lies as a special form of information. A lie is a person's preferred version of reality. You can imagine a silent "I wish" uttered before a lie. As in, "*I wish* I'm late because traffic was terrible." or "*I wish* I love your new haircut."

If you are talking with a person who is open to shifting perspectives, you can broach the subject of his or her lie. You can say, "I don't believe you," in response and leave it at that. Don't push the issue. If they are open to admitting their lie or bolstering belief, they will do so without more prodding from you.

We are taught as children that lies are very bad, which is a judgment, not a law of nature. Lies are everywhere. We are a creative species and we are adept at fabricating many layers of falsehood on top of truth. Fictional books, movies, children's stories, these are all lies too. Stop worrying about lies. They can't hurt you. The real trouble sits with a lack of integrity. Lies that allow for broken circles of integrity and lies that allow you to pretend you are in integrity when you are not, those things will hurt you.

## Compulsions

You will start to notice other people's beliefs too. When you are clear of emotional backlog and you aren't struggling with your own beliefs, you can hear nearly everyone's beliefs. At first, this might be hard to deal with. You may feel like you have to share your information about their beliefs with them. You may want to help them. In most cases, they won't be able to hear you. Telling them that their beliefs are illusions is like telling them gravity doesn't exist. The conversation will make no sense to them.

I had dinner with someone who kept talking about how she believed she wasn't smart enough. I'm the only one who heard her truth so loudly. The other people at the table found her to be a little caught up on something, but they couldn't put their finger on it. All I could hear was her compulsion to judge everyone's intelligence against her own. She talked about a movie she saw recently and about a problem she was having at work. Both stories were used as evidence that she was smart enough. I could tell that her belief had been a source of suffering for her throughout her life. She was preoccupied with being smart enough. I felt exhausted and on-edge listening to her. She probably felt the same way.

For a while it might seem like people are blatantly flaunting their beliefs. You can see their beliefs so clearly that it seems like they must be desperate to share them. Your ACC can start to scream *Do something!* You may convince yourself that you have to help people now that you can hear their beliefs. When you feel compelled to help people in this way, it's the same as any other compulsion. Your compulsions are based on your beliefs. Examine what's driving your need to point out other people's beliefs, do nothing, and use the experience to further calibrate your ACC.

Over time, you will find ease in hearing other people's beliefs and doing nothing. Those who get to a clear mind will be able to hear the truth in every conversation. After a while it becomes normal. If you grew up in a place that was very conservative and you never saw men go shirtless or women wearing short skirts, you might have a few weeks or months of surprise and adjustment as you learned what partly nude bodies look like. Then, you'd get used to it. Seeing skin would become routine over time. Hearing beliefs is similar. The truth shines through conversations as though it were uncovered intentionally. At first the truth is as startling as unexpected nudity. Over time it becomes routine and commonplace. Just like everyone has a naked body under their clothes, everyone has an intimate truth under their bolstering beliefs and fiction.

## Polite conversation

Once you know that polite conversation is fundamentally based on fiction and bolstering beliefs, it can be hard to know how to talk to people. Feel free to mostly listen and say little. Your powers of listening are stronger than ever when you aren't driven by beliefs and compulsions. You'll be amazed at how close you can feel to someone when you listen to them without filtering their words through your beliefs first.

When you do speak, stick to saying things that are both true and beneficial. Said another way, you can use speech to be entertaining, to give information, to connect to another person, or any other number of reasons. Notice when you start using speech to put others down, flaunt your abilities, or confess your deepest thoughts. Refrain from speaking when the topic is driven by a compulsion. If you are compelled to say something that is true but steps over the bounds of beneficial speech, then ask yourself what's going on for you. Where does this compulsion come from?

Conversation can be funny, kind, imaginative, and emotional. You can dredge up old feelings of pain, as long as the conversation stays beneficial. Conversation can include lies and pretense, as long as everyone knows that you are lying and pretending. Feel free to laugh as much as you want. Humans are hilarious. You can laugh at yourself or someone else, but do it with compassion and not with a sense of superiority. We are all in this together.

Allow yourself to follow others as they guide you in conversations. People will tell you a lot if you are willing to simply follow them through their thought process. Generally, there's no need to guide conversations when you don't have an agenda. When your goal is simply to connect, then do so with openness, warmth, and listening.

Business conversations, and business-like conversations at home, do have agendas. Be sure to tell your conversation partner what you hope to get out of the conversation when there is an agenda. Leave nothing to assumptions. Balance between following others in their thoughts and making sure that the agenda is accomplished. When your compulsions don't drive your conversations, you can be relaxed about listening and accomplishing goals. Your conversation partner is more likely to hear your points when you aren't compulsively driving the conversation where you want it to go.

The biggest difference, you may notice, is that there is no required format to your behavior or speech anymore. In the past, manners dictated how you are supposed to conduct yourself. Manners are not necessary. There is no correct order to who says what, or which words you are supposed to use. If you hold firm to your integrity, the rest takes care of itself. Authenticity is more valuable than manners. Speak and act with the intention of allowing your external expressions match your internal experience. Allow your internal experience to be gracious and accepting of whatever is.

You may discover that you stop engaging in your old behaviors. If, in conversation, you used to hide your agenda until the time was right, you may find that you choose to share your agenda upfront, or even refrain from having an agenda at all if the time is not right to share it. You may find that you skip the small talk. Connecting with people is the most powerful form of conversation that you can have, and you have to do very little talking to accomplish that. Listening to another person and contributing your truth is all it takes to connect.

## Relationships

Your relationships will change. It doesn't matter that you read this book or that you do any of the exercises in it. Your relationships will change because that's what relationships do. Couples married happily for 30 years will tell you that their relationship took on many different forms as their life progressed. The same marriage is not always the same relationship. Your relationship to your children, friends, parents, or the anonymous stranger will continuously change over the course of your life. This is a beautiful part of life, constantly evolving relationships.

You may talk about relationships as though there are certain types and that each has certain rules associated with it. Most people talk about the quintessential five types of relationships, parent/child, romantic love, friendship, stranger, and acquaintance. Instead of separating relationships out into these categories, consider that there is another way to look at relationships. A connection to a person, no matter what it's based in, constitutes a relationship. Everything else about that relationship is an agreement between the two people.

When your relationships are no longer driven by your beliefs and compulsions about what a certain type of relationship entails, you can make conscious decisions about your relationships. You can make conscious agreements with the other person so that you both know what's expected. Agreements can be changed at any time by either party.

This type of relationship building allows for constant personal growth without threatening the relationship.

Here's an example: Two friends Ali and Marie had known each other for nearly ten years. They met in school. After graduation, they made a habit of getting coffee or breakfast once a month or so. Ali watched Marie's cat when she went on business trips. They had an agreed structure to their friendship, an hour or two together to catch up monthly and the addition of small favors. They had mutual respect.

Marie began to see a boyfriend seriously for the first time since the two friends had met and the relationship between Ali and Marie changed. Marie was an extremely quiet person, and after she started dating someone, she seemed less likely to want to be social with Ali. Understandably, Marie was tired of being social after spending social time with her boyfriend. Marie instead called on Ali for practical matters like favors of rides to the airport or help with her cat, but didn't call on her for social time anymore. Ali got tired of being called only for favors, and she asked Marie to call her for entertainment activities, like a trip to the park instead. In effect, Ali changed their agreement. She was ok with doing Marie favors when Marie was willing to be social with her too, but if the relationship was going to be based solely on favors, then Ali wasn't willing to participate.

Relationships can be based on countless different things. Ali and Marie had a mutual respect that wouldn't be damaged if they spent less time together. However, if Ali had continued to do favors for Marie without telling her that she wasn't ok with it, then that lack of integrity could have damaged the relationship.

Without beliefs and compulsions blocking your ability to see what's going on in your life, you can begin to identity what your relationships are based on. You'll begin to see the unspoken agreements that you've made with other people. When you find that you no longer agree to those terms or to the basis of your relationship, then you need to have a discussion with the other person. The value of the relationship doesn't have to change, but the agreements must be discussed. Going along with an agreement (spoken or unspoken) that you no longer agree to is a surefire way to damage a relationship.

To keep all relationships healthy, be sure to broach any unspeakable topics that arise. When you have something on your mind and you aren't willing to talk about it, you create a barrier in that relationship. You don't have to discuss details, simply saying, "I have something on my mind that I've been keeping from you," can be enough. Sharing more might be better. Something as simple as, "I don't have as much fun with you right now as I used to. I'm not sure what's up with that." It might sound terrifying to be that honest with a friend or partner, but it can open a spectacularly intimate conversation as long as you use MindSET tools to stay out of reaction. It's fine if the other person goes into reaction. You know what to do about that. Nothing.

Make no expectations of your relationships. Expectations are very similar to beliefs. If you believe another person must treat you a certain way, or behave a certain way, then you have a belief that is destined to become a conflict. As you uncover beliefs, recognize that we tend to create a lot of them around how we believe other people are supposed to act toward us.

When others have expectations of you, you can tell them that you don't agree to that expectation. Talk through it and notice your feelings. You may discover that you have been unwittingly supporting others' expectations of you, even when you didn't agree. Stop fulfilling your side of the expectation in that relationship and the expectations fall away quickly.

Sometimes relationships end and that's ok too. It's important to stay in integrity even as a relationship is coming to a close. Acting out your emotions, saying things out of compulsion, and acting out of judgment will cause conflict for you. Remember, a relationship that ends well can begin again in the future on new terms. A relationship that ends poorly has little chance of ever reviving.

## Actions

Your actions are completely within your control. In the past, you may have felt as though your emotions were controlling your actions. Now, you see that it's your belief that controlled you. As you clear your beliefs and clean your net of emotional backlog, you will realize just how much control you have over your actions. You can do things you thought were impossible.

Many of the behaviors you have been attributing to your personality are present because of your beliefs. Without those beliefs, you are free to perform behaviors or stop doing them. It's your choice. I had maintained a belief about which jobs I was suited to. I had a belief that I wasn't a very good sales person. After I let go of a series of beliefs, I recognized that, not only was I a good salesperson, but I had a lot of examples of having successfully sold products, services, and ideas over the course of my career. Before clearing my beliefs, I thought I wouldn't be suited for a sales-type job. I realized, that I was capable of selling and I had a track record to prove it. I could do whatever I had the appetite to do.

When you are no longer limited by beliefs, you are limited only by appetite. If you wish to perform brain surgery, and you have the appetite to do so, then you will find a way to get from here to there. If you wish to reconcile with your estranged family, and you have the appetite to do it, then you will go from here to there. Anything you want to do, if you have the appetite, you will find a way to do it.

You may find that you still have compulsions and that they feel impossible to control. Compulsions are your most valuable key to finding more beliefs. When you have a compulsion or you find yourself unable to control your behavior, notice that. Follow it. Feel it. And when you find the belief, you can decide whether you want to keep it or let it go.

## Decisions

When you start crumbling the walls of your belief fortress, you have a lot more freedom to make decisions. You find yourself less compelled to act certain ways and you may stand in awe of how many options you have. It may seem that you have so many choices that it is impossible to make decisions. Your identity doesn't have to drive your choices anymore. Your fear of the unknown doesn't have to limit your options anymore. There are many things that may have weighed on your decision-making in the past. Now that you can see those as bolstering beliefs, you know that they aren't real limitations.

There are many ways that you limit your decision making ability when you are a slave to your bolstering beliefs. Now, you can recognize when you use one of these beliefs to limit your options. Uncertainty creates the discomfort feeling of unrest and makes you feel like you shouldn't move forward with an uncertain option, but you now know that uncertainty is just a feeling. Subscribing to authority causes you to blame your decisions on others, generally loved ones or an employer, but you now know that you are your only true authority. Your own identity can make you question whether a set of options is right for you, but you can see that you are not limited by superficial definitions of who you are. In the past you may have believed that your choices are limited by the resources you currently have, but now you see that resources are fungible. You resources are limited only by your appetite for finding more of what you need. You might have worried about making the wrong choice in the past, but now you understand that there are no right and wrong choices, there is only cause and effect. Any claim about making the right choice or the wrong choice is part of the illusion that perfection exists.

Robert Frost's Poem, The Road Not Taken describes a man standing at a fork in a path. He describes the two paths as being equal and he laments that he can't see where both lead. We do this every day. With an option between two choices, we lament that we can't know everything about the road not taken. What did we pass up? Was it better than the choice we took? It's impossible to know what a disregarded choice might have provided and so how do we choose?

If the man in Frost's poem could see further down one path, and the other path were obscured, this might have made his decision easier. We are deeply affected by what we do know about a choice. Now that you are aware of uncertainty, and the effect that it can have on the attractiveness of an option, you can start to ignore it. When dealing with two choices, ignore all uncertainty. Notice the discomfort, stay out of reaction, and assess what you do actually know about the choices. Ignore the unknowns.

Here's an example. My mother is looking to buy a new house. She's shopping for homes in different neighborhoods. Some are regular neighborhoods with single family homes where each person owns their own land and property. Some are like the condominium version of single family homes. An organization owns the land and the owners own the house. As my mom tries to decide which home to buy, she's struggling to compare apples and oranges. In one set of options, she owns the land, which is a value. In the other set of options she doesn't have to worry about the land, which is also a value to her since she is getting older and doesn't love yard work anymore. How do you compare the two?

It would be an easy mistake to start thinking about which house will have the best resale value and compare along those lines. Houses are an investment and the resale is a big part of any investment. It's a mistake to use resale as a factor in your decision making in this case. You have no idea how the housing market will change over time. You have no idea whether condo-like houses will be more or less attractive to buyers in the future. This is an unknown.

Instead, make decisions based on the information you have. You know the size of the home, the currently comparable prices, and how much you like the houses. You know whether you can afford the home easily or if you will need to make adjustments in your finances. It's hard to completely ignore the unknowns, but trying to use them in your decision making just invites illusion into the process.

When you stop fooling yourself with beliefs, you can see the clear cause and effect of your actions. If you buy the house that is a little bit out of your price range, you will have to scrimp other places in your budget, or find a way to make more money. Otherwise, you will go into debt. If you choose to buy the smaller, less expensive house, you may have to find hotels for guests when they visit. These are the natural consequences of your decisions. Ignoring these consequences or pretending that they aren't real will put you out of integrity.

Use cause and effect to determine what you desire. You might want a big expensive house, but you also want to have extra money for vacations. Recognize that having the big house makes vacations less affordable. Do you still want the big house if you will have to work longer hours to pay for it? Do you still want the big house if you only get to go on vacation every other year?

There are two things to consider when you are making decisions, your desire and your appetite. It's senseless to make decisions that you don't desire. Stop doing that. You can blame your decisions on other people or say that your hand was forced, but it's not the truth. In fact, every decision you've ever made, you made because you desired it. Your desires masquerade behind blame and barriers.

Your appetite will allow you to overcome challenges and reach your goals. If you don't have the appetite to follow through with a specific decision, then don't go that way. Moving forward without an appetite to keep going is a recipe for failure.

## Separateness

Nearly all suffering comes from the belief the you are separate from something that you wish to have. Suffering can also come from the worry that you could lose (be separated from) something that you currently have. Separateness is an illusion.

To end suffering, you can find a perspective in which you see how you are simply distant from the thing (or person) that you wish to have. Distance can be overcome with sufficient appetite.

A seemingly final example of being separated from someone occurs in death. It's human nature to mourn the loss of a loved one, but many people continue to mourn for extended periods, up to decades, after a particularly close person has died. When someone has died, it's important to notice the sensations and emotions that occur during mourning.

Your thoughts can deeply influence how you progress through mourning. Focusing on separateness leads to suffering. You cannot be separate from your loved one even after they are dead. They live with you, inside you, and you couldn't get rid of them if you wanted to. Benefit permanence allows you to have the benefits of this person even though you are distanced from them. Consider all of the things that this person set in motion during their life. Those things, in the present, are forever affected by them. You couldn't undo those actions if you wanted to. To feel close to a person who has passed, you can stop focusing on separateness, and shift your perspective to see how any separateness is an illusion. You cannot be separated from anyone.

Separateness is the primary source of pain associated with any loss or fear of loss. Death is an extreme example. You may feel separate from people or things. Those who suffer unrequited love are focused on the separateness that stands between them and their love object. Those who wish they could make more money are focused on the *lack* of money.

These problems can be overcome by accepting that separateness is an illusion.

Some self-help advice suggests that you can think your way to more money. This often doesn't work because you'll put money (or whatever your object of interest) on a pedestal and recognize it as a goal that has yet to be attained. You cannot get close to something while you see it as separate from you. Even if you do make a lot of money, it won't last, you'll find yourself without money again soon while you believe that it is separate from you. The suffering around money ends the moment you recognize that you were never separate from money. That feeling was an illusion all along. There are infinite ways for you to connect with money on a daily basis.

When you feel separate from another person you will create separateness between you and them. If you notice that you have a feeling of separateness in a relationship you can decide to let that illusion go, and without changing anything else, your relationship will be immediately closer. In your mind, the relationship will feel closer. Then in your actions, you will have nuanced behaviors that increase your closeness. Remember, empathy transmits feelings. When you feel separate from someone, you transmit that separateness to them too. They feel it. When that illusion of separateness originates with you, the other person has no chance of overcoming it. You are the only one who can let it go.

Dissolve separateness by translating it into distance first. Whatever is causing you to suffer, recognize that you are distanced from it. Then work to shift your perspective. Redefine what it would take to feel less distanced. You may discover that your suffering is relieved simply by seeing the situation differently. Perspective shift can be a powerful exercise to relieve suffering caused by illusions of separateness.

# Returning Home

You have been on a hero's journey. If you have completed the journey, and let go of your key belief, then you are ready to return home. You will be unencumbered by the past, and ready to join your loved ones again.

First, you received a call to conflict when you found yourself compelled to act because you were experiencing the pain of being in reaction. You refused the call at first, by denying that it was your problem. You saw the problem as someone else's problem. Through the magic of MindSET you got out of reaction long enough to realize that you had a hand in the problem too. You saw that it was your responsibility to end the conflict and no one could do it for you. As you followed your feelings, pain and suffering from the past came forward. You went through the trials of emotion and found insight into your beliefs. You discovered that your identity was at stake. Could you let go of your beliefs? You questioned whether you would be the same person without them.

Now, it's time to go back to your life. You are lighter, stronger, and more able to handle the challenges you face. You will embark on this journey again, many times. Each conflict will be a new call to another hero's journey.

Reading this book is not enough. You will have to do the exercises and consciously apply the things you learned to your daily life. No one can do this for you and no one can make it easier. You can choose to gather a MindSET Group around you so that you can learn along with others. Most people find it imperative to have others nearby who also understand feelings, awareness, authenticity, and separateness. It is incredibly valuable to be able to tell another person your experiences, especially when they are going through the same changes. Your life can change.

The world is shifting. Job applications often include a request that new hires embody corporate values which tend to include integrity, authenticity, and teamwork. These notions are no longer on the fringe. Soon, you'll be in the minority if you haven't done the personal development that allows for you to see through bolstering beliefs. To be authentic, you have to recognize the difference between pretending and truth. To live in integrity, you have to be conscious of the moments when you slip out of integrity. The only way to live with any values is to be aware of the fact that sometimes you fail to live within your chosen values. Human nature includes mistakes. If you think you are always in integrity, you are in denial.

As you develop awareness, you will clearly see parts of the world that seem ugly. Good people lie a lot. Justice is an illusion. Death, war, and conflict are fundamental parts of human existence. These look like ugly things that need to be fixed, until you see that they have always existed. There has always been a dark side and a light side to the world. You can't have one without the other. Humans are, by nature, both dark and light.

Rainbows move along with the movements of the person viewing them. The rest of the world reacts to you as well. You influence your own outcomes more than you may realize. The beauty of the world sits with the beholder - that's you. Your body allows you to sense the uplifting (beauty, love, wonder) and the cheerless (rawness, melancholy, distress). Your awareness allows you to choose the dark or light side of each experience you have. Ideally you will find a perspective that allows you to see both light and dark simultaneously. Seeing one without the other is an illusion; dark and light always come together.

You will discover that all emotions are wonderful. No emotion is painful when it is experienced in the moment through a clear net. Disgust, sadness, and even anger are colorful variations of the way you can feel. Emotional pain comes from emotional constipation, not from the emotion. Just like with intestinal constipation, perfectly good food can cause severe pain.

You will have to take time over the next few months to clear out your net so that you can experience pain-free emotion. Remember to use noticing as your main tool. Notice, without judgment, each emotion that arises for you. Don't ask why, just feel it. Your friends and family might wonder why you are dredging up old issues long past. Share the idea of emotional constipation with them, if they are confused. Intestinal cleanse is a popular health craze, so they might understand through that analogy. As long as you know that you are productively getting through the emotions in your net, you can rest easy in spending time crying, angry, or irritated. It gets better. It gets so much better.

If you get overwhelmed with the process of noticing, ACC calibration, or emotional net clearing, give up. Pushing these things on yourself when you aren't ready doesn't do you any good. This medicine only works when you can ease through it. Not when you force your way through it. Stop trying so hard. Come back to it when you feel it pulling you, not when you have to push yourself.

# Conclusion

I wish you all the best. Some say the meaning of life is to spend your time on earth finding the peace that lives between the light and dark sides of human nature. You may find it and lose it again many times. Although suffering is an ever present law of nature, you can minimize your experience of it by managing your relationship to separateness. You can significantly increase your ease of life by living in integrity. Those are the two most powerful forces on the planet.

As you retire old beliefs and learn to live in a world that is not bound by barriers, you discover that life is full of freedom. Conflicts that were once devastating become surmountable. Life is easy. Integrity is the only part of life where you will need to continually work hard. You will have to keep up a daily practice of keeping your desires and appetites aligned. You will follow through with the things you started or you will find a way to retire the circle when it no longer makes sense to close it.

New conflicts all but disappear when you stop making new beliefs. You can learn to live in the world where there are no perfect answers and no concrete reasons for anything. You can give up the illusion of separateness to accept that you are distantly connected to everything. When you can do this, you will find that your expectations dissolve and they are replaced with compassion and hope. Nothing seems impossible.

Since much of the world is an illusion, here's to making it one you want to experience!

# ABOUT THE AUTHOR

Nicole Gravagna, PhD is a neuroscientist who learned about human behavior long after she learned about the brain. She devotes her time to mentoring college students and early career professionals. She is an engaging public speaker on the topics of career development, entrepreneurship, change management, and conflict. Nicole is also co-author of Venture Capital for Dummies. You can find more of her writing on Quora.com where she was named a Quora Top Writer 2016. She has been published in Forbes, Inc., and The New York Observer. She is a regular contributor to Huffington Post and StartupNation.